Ex Libris

Lowell R. Kantzer

THE DIMENSIONS OF LIBERTY

THE

DIMENSIONS

OF

LIBERTY

Oscar and Mary Handlin

The Belknap Press of
☆ Harvard University Press
Cambridge, Massachusetts
1961

Library of Congress Catalog Card Number 61–16694
PRINTED IN THE UNITED STATES OF AMERICA

To the Memory of
Arthur Wilson Page
(1883–1960)
Friend of Liberty and of Learning

CONTENTS

THE DIMENSIONS OF LIBERTY

INTRODUCTION

THE preservation of liberty is the preeminent problem of our times. For the past half century a gnawing fear has crept through the Western world: the precious gains in freedom that once seemed destined to spread toward horizons of indefinite extension now appear to be threatened by hostile forces of overwhelming power. There is danger not simply that the area within which liberty is cherished may cease to expand, but also that it may actually contract.

The peril gains force from the fact that the most insidious assaults come in unrecognizable forms, sometimes themselves bearing the banner, liberty. In the confusing issues of the past fifty years it has often been difficult to make out who were the champions and who were the foes of freedom. And the difficulty has not been one of semantics only. Time and again, movements which got under way with the intention of unchaining the people, achieved the unanticipated, tragic result of enmeshing them firmly in new bonds. Many thinkers wonder, with Isaiah Berlin, whether the ideal of freedom was any more than a perishable "late fruit of our declining capitalist civilization," one unknown to earlier societies and which "posterity will regard with curiosity, even sympathy, but little comprehension."[1]

Hence the confusion both about the meaning of the term and about the nature of the condition, liberty. Is the man free who suffers no external restraints but can find no employment? Or is he free if the state compels him to participate in a scheme for social security? Is there a gain in freedom if the termination of colonialism simply exchanges foreign for native despots? Are the masses free who choose dictatorship?

Hence also the confusion about the causes and consequences of liberty — whatever the meaning of the term. Are men made happier, wiser, wealthier as a result of having it; or do they seek it in order to attain such goals? Is freedom an aid or a deterrent to economic growth; and, conversely, does material well-being stimulate or impede the quest for it? How is liberty related to the strength of nations and their capacity for survival?

To all such questions, the political philosophy of the past offers no clear answers; and the tests of present-day experience are painfully imperfect.

The want of guiding standards is particularly critical in the United States. Through most of their history, Americans tended to take their liberties for granted as the products of natural, almost providential, forces destined to spread everywhere. At this juncture in their experience, however, doubts as to the validity of those liberties are widely expressed within the nation and outside it. There is urgent need for a formulation that will outline the central issues and at least expose the alternatives which the citizens of a Republic must face as they make the choices that will shape their future.

Such considerations moved Harvard University in 1958 to establish the Center for the Study of the History of Liberty in America. The mandate of the Center was to undertake a dispassionate and scholarly examination of the elements that brought the distinctive patterns of American freedom into being.

The focus of attention upon a single nation, the United States, rested on the premise that study of the free society which developed there would yield conclusions of universal import. But the selection of this as the field of the Center's inquiries did not imply any prejudgment either concerning the uniqueness of its experience or the superiority of its development. Any meaningful conclusions about the nature of liberty in the modern world will necessarily call for reasoned comparisons with other countries. From time to time, the Center will undertake carefully planned pieces of research at critical points in the analysis of the problem, in the hope that what occurred elsewhere will throw light on what happened in the United States.

There is a more serious danger in treating the United States as if it were a coherent entity, deliberately moving toward goals self-consciously perceived. It was not. Always it was a vast conglomerate of diverse regions and populations; and the forces that shaped it were rarely the products of deliberate decisions.

From the very start, the country contained offshoots of Dutch as well as English enterprise; throughout its history it drew its citizenry from a multitude of sources. Already in the seventeenth century, there were characteristic differences between Massachusetts and Virginia, the seeds of which would be carried westward with the moving frontier. The course of settlement brought Americans into a variety of physiographic regions; and the accommodation of law and social institutions to the conditions of the Mississippi delta was not that of the Great Plains. Dissimilarities in the rate and in the character of economic change made regional variations still more complex. The Gulf states differed from those of New England not only in climate and in resources but also in the timing of industrialization and of its concomitant effects.

As a result, Americans organized themselves in communities so different as to fall into no simple scheme of classification. Chicago in 1960 was not the same as Los Angeles, to say nothing of Memphis or Elmira or Butte or Dutchess County; and none was what it had been fifty years earlier. Furthermore, all contained a complex of subcultures. Carpenters and machinists, wheat growers and cotton farmers, bankers and clerks, doctors and teachers, Negroes and Yankees, Jews and Crackers, made their own responses to their environment, had their own interests, and led their own lives.

Every generalization about the Americans must, therefore, be qualified by a consciousness of the reality of these differences, particularly in relation to the problems of liberty. The historical record is vivid when it deals with abrupt changes; it takes less notice of forces that operate slowly and imperceptibly. Yet, in the development of law and of social institutions generally, inertia is as important as conscious decision. Deeply rooted habits of thought and action, assumptions about the nature of man, society, and the state remain quiescent over long periods, shift with glacial slowness, and only occasionally erupt into visibility. To trace their evolution one must follow long chains of cause and effect through adjustments to the environment of diverse regions back to European sources.

Therein lies one of the values of the present undertaking. Precisely because the United States did not enjoy the relative continuity and uniformity of France or Sweden, or even England, its history may be especially relevant to the present and future condition of liberty. It confronted early what is coming to be the problem of all modern men, preservation of the ability of people of dissimilar origins to act together under dissimilar conditions.

And, despite all the differences among them, the Americans did share the common experience of liberty. Even before a national state gave it political form, there was a national identity, in the establishment of which the problem of being free played a significant part.

The focus on that whole experience will offset the danger implicit in concentrating the analysis upon a single nation. This procedure will offer an opportunity for intensive examination of the many different phenomena related to men's ability to exist in freedom. Liberty, however it is defined, is a complex, not a simple condition. Whether it thrives or not depends upon the character of the government, upon the system of production, upon the order of society, and upon the beliefs men hold about themselves and their place in the universe. These circumstances and the interconnections among them can best be understood in a single national context.

Liberty acquired strength in the United States from the fact that it did not develop simply within a single sphere of life. Rather, it permeated every aspect of the behavior of the whole society. It will not be understood other than through an awareness of its multiple dimensions.

Among all the other ways in which freedom manifested itself in the United States it is possible to recognize three general forms of particular importance. American freedom possessed a political aspect. It depended upon the development, since the seventeenth century, of traditions of free government on every level; and it drew support from systems of ideas and patterns of action through which those traditions operated.

Liberty was also social in character. A significant degree of mobility inhibited the rigid stratification of the population. The looseness of the social order helped to develop a sense of the worth of the individual and gave people of every sort a conviction that they had an important stake in the freedom of the communities in which they lived.

Finally, the evolution of voluntary religious, economic, cultural, and philanthropic organizations offered alternatives to state action in matters in which unanimity did not prevail. The highly diverse elements of which the nation was composed could seek their own ends without fear of interference. Secure in the knowledge that the role of the government did not encompass every aspect of life, Americans created an apparatus of free institutions with which each group of them could seek its own goals without coercion.

The development of these dimensions of liberty forms a vast and hitherto relatively neglected realm of American history that the Center proposes to investigate. It hopes to assemble the historical materials necessary for a comprehension of the total problem so that the concrete data of the past may supply a firm foundation for conclusions relevant to the present and the future.

Out of its research there will ultimately come a long work of synthesis that will tell the story of the continuing development of American liberty. But no single book could hope to encompass the subject as a whole; nor could any individual aspire himself to assemble all the materials bearing upon it. It therefore seemed necessary to enlist the aid of a corps of scholars whose talents can be focused upon specific sectors of the central problem. The Center proposes to commission a large number of autonomous monographs of various lengths, each to deal with an aspect of the subject and each to be the product of independent research and individually written. These works will be valuable in themselves and will also contribute data to the final synthesis.

The magnitude of the effort to be expended in this process called immediately for a preliminary analysis that would survey the whole subject, outline the significant problems, and reveal what had already been done by earlier scholars and what yet remained to be accomplished. Involved in this task was the construction of a broad framework that would comprehend the whole subject. The issue of liberty was, after all, bound in with almost every phase of the history of the United States. The problems of political organization, social mobility, and voluntary association were central to the American experience. The preliminary analysis thus had to arrive at judgments of what was or was not relevant. In doing so it reached tentative conclusions, which have a

general interest, on the nature of liberty itself. The results
are presented in this volume.

The analysis did not take as its point of departure a
theoretical definition of liberty. The historians of ideas have
counted fully two hundred senses in which the word has
been used.[2] It was not necessary or desirable to establish
an a priori commitment to one of these definitions; the
concern of the Center is not the abstract meaning of the
term, but rather analysis and description of the operations
in the United States of what men have considered a free
society.

The analysis therefore began with an inquiry about what
liberty had actually meant in the life of Americans in the
past. That inquiry yielded nine propositions or hypotheses,
the validity of which future studies by the Center will test.

    I. Liberty has meant not the negation but the proper
use of power.

    II. Power was to be organized and exercised within
defined procedures.

    III. There were limits beyond which power ought not to
be used.

    IV. Power might be used for some ends but not for others.

    V. Important spheres of social action were to be left in
the United States to voluntary associations without
the capacity for coercion.

    VI. These might not however act in a conspiratorial
fashion.

    VII. Power might be used to increase the wealth of the
nation because just modes of distribution assured the
equal access of all to it.

    VIII. The social structure of the United States encouraged
social mobility.

    IX. Efforts in the past to restrict the scope of mobility
have not been successful.

To the extent that the studies to be commissioned by the Center will throw light upon the accuracy of these propositions they will contribute to an understanding of the nature of liberty in the United States.

Meanwhile, the volume which follows offers a tentative exposition of the reasoning which entered into the formulation of these propositions. As such it may have independent value as a statement of the issues to all those interested in the problems of liberty.

☆ I ☆

LIBERTY
AND
POWER

T HE free man," wrote Helvetius, "is a man who is not in irons, nor imprisoned in jail, nor terrorized like a slave by fear of punishment." Therein, he echoed an earlier definition by Hobbes: "Liberty, or freedom, signifieth, properly, the absence of opposition. . . . *A FREEMAN is he, that in those things, which by his strength and wit he is able to do, is not hindered to do what he has a will to do.*"[1]

These statements express one of the central assumptions of Western political theory in the past three centuries. Liberty from this point of view is the antithesis of the power of others; the one exists when the other is absent. Freedom therefore is a condition at which the individual arrives by safeguarding himself against compulsion or the threat of compulsion. The prototype of the man who is completely free is Robinson Crusoe who inhabits a world in which no superior commands and no law binds him.

The philosophers and historians who have sustained this conception have described the condition of liberty in negative terms. They have sought to understand its development through analysis of the means by which men have defended themselves and their rights against restraint. Since, in modern times, the most compelling engines of coercion have been those organized in government, the history of liberty has been written largely as a succession of episodes and trends through which people have learned to ward off interference by the state.[2]

This conception of liberty has by no means won the assent of all modern philosophers; other definitions fit into a line of speculation that reaches from Plato to Whitehead and that gives the term quite a different meaning.[3] But the negative view has supplied the basis from which almost all historians have treated the development of liberty in the past three hundred years.

In the discussion that follows it is not essential to pass upon the validity of the negative concept as an abstract philosophical proposition.[4] But it is essential to judge the adequacy of that concept for the purpose of describing how people acted under conditions that might be designated as free.

The image of the absence of restrictions is certainly useful in describing some phases of the development of institutions conducive to freedom in the United States. The struggle against governmental restraints helped to establish freedom of speech and of the press, and religious and academic liberty. And much of the literature of the subject is devoted to investigations of the course and outcome of those struggles.[5]

But their negative character restricts the utility of these works. They treat liberty as the ability of the individual to act in the absence of external restraints; and they therefore deal primarily with those factors, particularly in the realm of constitutional law, which limit the capacity of the government to exercise such restraints. Indeed, almost the whole of this literature can be classified in terms of the relevant articles of the federal constitution on which the legal defense of such liberty has hung.

This narrow conception circumscribes the subject in a way that excludes critical aspects of it. The books written from this point of view deal primarily with infringements upon liberty — that is, with what liberty is not, rather than with what it is. They are therefore incapable of shedding light upon many of the most important questions raised by American development.

The various available histories of the freedom of the press, for instance, have concentrated almost exclusively upon the threats of governmental censorship and control. Important as these accounts are, their emphasis is misplaced; and the resultant simplification of a complex process may be misleading. Even had these treatments been broad enough to include restraints from other than governmental sources, they would still have been deficient. During the last century, at least, the most serious dangers to the liberty of American journalism have not emanated from governmental interference. The influence of private groups, limitations on the access to news, and the process of consolidation have more effectively inhibited free expression through the medium of newspapers than has interference by the state or by other coercive means.[6]

Significant issues thus remain, in the analysis of which the criterion of external compulsion offers little assistance. For instance, reporters are less free to express their own opinions than professors, not because they are more subject to control from without, but because a newspaper is a different kind of institution from a university. To understand the difference it is necessary to know why the property rights of publishers and college trustees evolved along dissimilar lines and why an intricate social development has given the press one status in the community and the college another.

In any case, a survey of successive incidents of repression hardly offers the ground for understanding the source of the strength to resist. The development of religious freedom offers an example. At the establishment of the colonies, the state exercised rigid supervision over worship. For a century and a half, its capacity to interfere in this realm did not diminish; the history of that period is one of repeated assaults upon the liberty of conscience. Yet, by 1760, before any significant changes in the law or in the character of government, that liberty was widely accepted. An account of the resistance to earlier attacks will by no means explain the tolerance of the mid-eighteenth century which was the product of altogether different social and cultural forces.[7]

It is furthermore impossible to deal with conflicts among liberties if those are measured simply by the absence of restraint. How can one weigh the freedom of the press against the right to privacy of the individuals treated in it, or against the right to strike of its employees, or against the ability of a dissatisfied group to boycott it? Was it a loss to freedom if the antitrust laws curtailed the liberties of the monopolist in order to extend those of his customers? Was it a gain if the Scopes trial deprived a teacher of the capacity to choose what he would teach and confirmed the capacity of parents to choose what their children would learn? By the criterion of the absence of restraint, the most that can be said is that these cases involve a gain in the liberties of some and a loss in those of others. One cannot proceed thence to a judgment of whether the consequence is a general increase or shrinkage of freedom. Within this viewpoint no society can be termed free or unfree as a whole; the Nazi Reich and Jeffersonian America were each free in some respects and unfree in others.[8]

The conception of liberty as the absence of restraint focuses attention on fragmented areas of social experience as occasional threats of interference arise within them. But to treat freedom of speech, of the press, or of religion in isolation obscures the common social context that influenced them all and that gave each its meaning. To define liberties as unconnected negatives upon compulsion rules out of consideration the problem many men consider most pertinent of all, that of describing the attributes that make a society free. A larger, more positive conception of freedom must supply the basis for doing so.

The definition of liberty as the absence of restraint was the product of peculiar historical conditions. The term itself has had a shifting rather than a constant connotation; and although its negative meaning may be traced, as an idea, as far back as Aristotle, the emphasis upon that meaning is the product of the peculiar context of the eighteenth and nineteenth centuries. An analysis of the way in which the word was then used will prepare the ground for further consideration of the adequacy of the negative conception.

Liberty in that two-hundred-year period became the justification for a concerted attack upon a system of particularized privileges inherited from the past. The system then assaulted, and generally designated feudalism, actually was a complex order or hierarchy of rights and privileges, among them, the prerogatives attached to the Crown, as well as the powers vested in estates, in the church, in municipal and other corporations, and in individuals.

Such powers were not comprehensive or general: they were rather particularized in the sense that they were attached to differentiated groups or statuses. The privileges of men, corporations, or estates were not identical. Each was ascribed such powers as were appropriate to its rank or location in the total social order. And all the available instruments of coercion were dedicated to the preservation of those graduated powers which, from a later point of view, were "a general nuisance."[9]

Against these powers, discontented underprivileged social groups waged a long struggle, which often began by questioning a particular privilege but which frequently proceeded to a challenge of the propriety of privilege in general. The process created a bulwark of positive guarantees against the earlier abuses of power. The strategy of the conflict was necessarily negative, dedicated as it was to the eradication of practices deeply rooted in tradition, law, and politics.

In the protest against privilege, men appealed for freedom by fastening upon the only general sense of the term in the seventeenth century, that which distinguished persons who occupied a servile condition from those who did not. Villeins, slaves, and servants were personally unfree because they were dependent on the will and subject to the authority of a master; free men were not in this manner dependent. As a result, in the struggle against privilege, freedom came to hold the primary meaning of resistance to coercion. An era that was, above all, anxious to unbind the individual from the fetters that limited his capacity to act tended to define liberty in Helvetius' terms, as antithetical to the power of others.

Our own distance from the immediate issues of the struggle against feudalism reveals the inadequacy of the negative conception of liberty. The relation of the individual to the compulsion or the threat of compulsion that hangs over him is not the sole consideration in establishing his freedom.

The jail is certainly not a free society; nor are those confined in it free men. A variety of conditions exist within the prison walls. There are individuals for whom the bars are the dividing line between liberty and servitude. Others accept the conditions of the unfree society in which they live. They cease to be conscious of the warders, acquiesce in the restraints, and achieve a placid, secure existence within the general terms of their confinement. Such men do not gain freedom by their release; often they are bewildered on the outside by the very loss of the rules according to which they had learned to behave.[10]

The worlds of slavery and the concentration camps reveal the same inadequacy of the negative view of liberty. It would be mockery of the term to consider those societies free. Yet their constraints are impersonal and remote and are transmitted to the individual inmate in such overwhelmingly absolute forms that they often become his own way of life. The overseer or the guard acquire a paternal majesty from the circumstance that they provide the sole elements of order and security in the existence of their charges. The slaves remain slaves though they learn to obey without the flourish of the whip.[11]

There are unfree societies in which restraint is hardly felt. George Orwell and Aldous Huxley have imagined the kind of social order in which subjugation to a servile condition was so deeply ingrained that compulsion became unnecessary. There, government by clubs and firing squads is not merely inhumane but inefficient. Instead, the members of an all-powerful executive "control a population of slaves who do not have to be coerced, because they love their servitude." The criterion of negative liberty — the absence of governmental or other restraints — would offer no measurement of the lack of liberty of the Proles or the Alphas and Epsilons.[12]

The rigid rules of the historic monastic orders or of the disciplined party cell also have a binding quality which does not depend upon immediate compulsion. Yet it would be misleading to conceive of these as free societies. Entrenched habits of mind can produce an acceptance or dependence upon a rigid order that deprives the individual of the ability to make choices. One can conceive of a perfectly competitive market, in which there is such an equal distribution of power that no firm can do anything but follow the single path of action that is alone consistent with avoiding failure. Such a situation would lead to stasis; no one would have liberty to act other than as he had to. Any perfect equilibrium immobilizes those confined in it with no external restraint whatever.

On the other hand, coercion need not destroy the freedom of the individual, nor does restraint in itself make a society unfree. There have been slaves who enjoyed more liberty than their masters. The long tradition of jail literature that reaches down from Epictetus or from Boethius in his cell is evidence of the ability of men to withdraw to an inner "freedom lying beyond circumstance."[13] And the hospital, the sanitarium, and the school are constrained societies in which freedom is measurable not by the severity or laxity of the rules but by their genuine purpose. The individual bound by a compulsion neurosis may be less free outside the asylum than in it.[14] These instances demonstrate the inadequacy of the idea of liberty as purely the negation of external restraints. A broader conception is necessary to take account of the complexity of the problem.

Wherein is the Prole unfree, or the prisoner? Not merely in the restraints or the fears of restraint which to some degree bind all humans! The essence of their condition must be otherwise described.

The philosophers who stated their definitions in terms of the absence of restraint could not leave the abstract proposition in that bare form. Their explications went farther. The plain and acknowledged matter of fact, wrote Hume in describing the freedom of everyone who is not a prisoner and in chains, is that "by liberty we can only mean *a power of acting or not acting* . . . ; that is if we choose to remain at rest, we may, if we choose to move, we also may." In doing so he focused his definition on the positive element of choice. And Jonathan Edwards, for whom liberty was the absence of "hindrence or impediment," explained that in common speech that meant "the power, opportunity, or advantage that anyone has to do as he pleases."[15]

These thinkers thus had to introduce an additional element to make their conception of liberty as the absence of restraint conform to the actualities of the real world. They distinguished between the power of the individual which was the necessary condition enabling him to act and his freedom which was the sufficient condition. The prisoner had the power to walk, but bars deprived him of the liberty to do so. Of such men Hobbes said, "Whilest they are in prison, or restrained, with walls or chains" it is proper to say "they are not at liberty." On the other hand a legless man had liberty to move about but lacked the power. "When the impediment of motion, is in the constitution of the thing itself," Hobbes continued, it is proper to say it wants not the liberty, but rather, "the power to move, as when a man is fastened to his bed by sickness."[16]

Two crucial objections invalidate this distinction. It is possible to conceive abstractly of a kind of liberty that exists in the absence of the power to exercise it, as for example, that of men to walk to the moon or that of starving laborers not to accept the contract proferred by the only available employer. No external restraint prevents them from so doing. But in fact such freedom never leads to action and therefore never can be witnessed. The liberty to walk to the moon or to sign a contract becomes consequential to its possessor and to others only when it is associated with the ability to use it. History which is a record of events that occurred, not of those that can be conceived, can therefore take cognizance of the development of liberty only insofar as it was capable of being used, that is, only in some more affirmative sense than the absence of restraint.

Furthermore, external restraint is not the independent variable that Hobbes makes of it. The capacity of the bars to hold the prisoner is not intrinsic or self-defined but is dependent upon the limits of his power. If he were strong enough or possessed the proper instruments he could break forth. Such restraints themselves are only a reflection of the individual's lack of power. Conversely, the legless man's lack of power is not so absolute but that he could not be liberated by a set of crutches.

Liberty must be interpreted in the broader sense, as embracing the two conditions Hobbes differentiated. That was why John Dewey, from an altogether different point of departure, observed that "freedom from restriction" was "only a means to a freedom which is power."[17] However the concept could be viewed in the abstract, in the concrete, liberty has been susceptible of description only in terms of the power or ability to do.[18]

The measure of the lack of freedom is the lack of power. The prisoner or the slave is recognizable not so much by the restraints which bind him as by the inability to act and to cause others to act. The shackles and bars may contribute to his incapacity but they are not sufficient to describe or explain it.

Conversely, the free man is one who has power to act and to cause others to act. The liberty of Robinson Crusoe is measurable not in the lack of a ruler over him but in the extent of his power to do what he wished. The patient in the hospital remains free to the degree that he retains the ability to act within the constraints that he accepts. His liberty inheres in the power he retains.

It may be, as Mortimer Adler maintains, that beyond the immense variety of theories of liberty there is a common understanding that liberty in general consists of the ability or power of some sort to act in some way for some result.[19] It requires no philosophical commitment, however, to accept as the most useful mode of describing the liberty of the individual in society, the extent of his power and its relation to the power of others.

Liberty in operation consists, then, not in the negation, but in the use, of power. The liberty of the bishop, of the factory owner, of the union are most adequately described not in terms of the amount of restraint to which they are subject but in terms of the extent of their power to exercise an office, to control property, or to bargain collectively. Liberty of the press and of religion are most readily measured by the capacity of men to write and worship as they wish. Conflicts among liberties are best understood as conflicts among discordant powers, for the freedom of one man necessarily involves the capacity to move others.

Power, in this sense, comprehends a variety of types of influence; it is possible to refer meaningfully to spiritual power, economic power, and political power. The bishop who has the ability to excommunicate a communicant; the owner of the only factory in town who can dismiss an employee; the labor union which can strike — all have power, or freedom, although of different sorts.[20]

In the actual operations of society, balance among these varieties of capacities for action arises out of the mutual interdependence of those who exercise them. The bishop will hesitate to excommunicate a large or influential portion of his flock; the employer, to fire a hand who has the support of a union; the union, to strike against a corporation with great resources. The power, or liberty, of one is a restraint upon the power, or liberty, of the other. A social order is viable to the extent that various kinds of power can coexist.

Among these it is desirable to distinguish that type of power which rests upon force. The ability to coerce *vi et armis*, cannot readily be balanced except by the counteruse of force. The individual who is excommunicated or dismissed or who suffers from a strike has alternatives; however painful the choice may be, he still can decide whether to resist or yield. The person at whom a gun is pointed or on whom a tax is levied has no such choice, unless he himself possesses force.

This ultimate capacity for coercion has, in Western society, also borne a sacred quality. To take a human life, to draw blood, to maim a body created in God's image was offensive not merely to the precepts of a code but also to awesome inhibitions fed from deep emotional and religious sources. Violence, the use of force, was tolerable only when sanctified by some respected authority. The tradition of kingship as a paternal rule that made bloodshed legitimate reflected the sacred character of force.[21]

It is not necessary to pursue that abstract argument; it is enough to point out that Western practice always recognized the distinction between violence and other forms of power. Force has been the ultimate coercive measure, to which appeals from other types could be made, but from which no appeal was possible. Hence the insistence in Western society that force be marshaled entirely within the communal order of the state, which is the embodiment of political power.

The eighteenth- and nineteenth-century struggle against feudal practices not only defined liberty as the antithesis of power, but in doing so narrowed the conception of power to political power. The tactics of disputation which then emphasized the negative thus doubly obscured the original and fuller meaning of the word.

Earlier the term liberty was more likely to be used in the plural than in the singular and it was synonymous not only with freedom, but also with privilege, franchise, and license. The liberties of a municipality were the districts subject to its authority as well as the privileges of some of its residents; a person admitted to the freedom of a city or a corporation received access to its privileges and immunities; a freeman was an individual of defined rank and power. "The Lord Jesus," declared a Massachusetts document of 1641, "hath given to . . . all the people of god . . . full libertie to gather themselves into a Church Estaite."[22]

The usage of the seventeenth century referred to the capacity for action in a multitude of spheres. The state, as the custodian of force, the ultimate power, was in a position to confirm and support each particular liberty or power through explicit grants or through the recognition of custom. The colonial charters, and the European practice of the seventeenth century recognized that people occupied different grades in a stratified society and that their liberties varied accordingly.[23]

The opponents of the particularized liberties or privileges of the past, in their great debate, argued that the state ought not to act as it did because liberty lay in the absence of restraint. But they did not wish to eliminate all use of power or to destroy all capacity for compulsion; and they never hesitated to use force, once they themselves controlled it.

Their inconsistency was symptomatic; for the reality of their situation which led them to seek positive ends through politics often contradicted their rhetoric, laden as that was with arguments aimed against an older organization of power. And the dilemma was as acute in the United States, where only the shreds of the old practices had been transplanted, as it was in Europe where the system of privilege survived into the eighteenth century practically intact.

A meaningful definition of liberty therefore will not emerge simply from the analysis of the writings by Americans about it. Despite all the eloquence of the frequent appeals against one aspect or another of state action there was no serious questioning in the United States of the propriety of the exercise of the ability to coerce. Anarchism as a philosophical doctrine has been attractive only on the eccentric fringes of society; it has not detracted from the widespread acceptance of the necessity and desirability of compulsion in human affairs. Liberty has developed in America not in opposition to force but as a pattern of ways in which force was to be used.

To comprehend American liberty in a more positive sense, therefore, it will be essential to view it as an attribute of the way of life of the American people. Only thus will one understand how the conception of it has changed from time to time, why zeal for its defense has waxed and waned, and what values have influenced the relation among specific liberties. That demands an analysis, in as many dimensions as possible, of the extent to which the actual functioning of American society in the past three hundred years has generated free institutions and has left room for a way of life of which liberty has been a part.

American freedom seems most comprehensible in terms of three primary assumptions about the modes of coercion: first, that political power ought to be organized and exercised within defined procedures; second, that there are limits beyond which such power ought not to be used; and, third, that such power may be used for some ends and not for others. An investigation of these assumptions will supply a basis for further consideration of the realms of liberty not so directly related to the use of force.

THE
PROCEDURES
FOR
THE EXERCISE
OF POWER

THE wilderness challenged the deeply rooted restraints of all the Europeans who ventured into it. Here, removed from traditional institutions and habits, man could stand all-powerful and entirely free, if he wished to. He did not wish to.

What was to stay his hand if he chose to shoot a lonely Indian in the forest or to run off with the property of others or even, in extremes, if he chose to resort to the cannibalism by which the strong survived at the expense of the weak? Only the firmer impulse to resist the temptations of power and the determination to vest the capacity for coercion in safe communal forms.

Unlimited power was no power at all; unlimited liberty no liberty. In the absence of restraints, all men were potential victims; no one was free in his person or property. Hence the driving anxiety at Jamestown and at every successive frontier to establish the binding rules to govern the use of force. Only thus could men be sure of that measure of regularity they called law and escape the bloody alternative of the feud. It will take extensive research to explain why they sought to guide themselves by established procedures. At this point, it is possible only to describe by what procedures they attempted to create that order without which there would be no liberty for anyone.

For more than a century Americans experimented, without knowing that they did so, with the ways of formulating those rules. The governors, from Smith to Berkeley, who held power by the authority of the Crown, were individuals and, although they took counsel from those around them, in the last analysis acted by their own will. They were like the Oriental or European potentates who were themselves the law and who exacted obedience through a personal control of force, sanctified by respect based upon tradition.[1]

The colonists, however, were unwilling to be simply victims, "bound to submit without sound or movement" to a law that reflected the will of a master, who could dispose of the "lives and properties at his will and pleasure, in a manner so arbitrary that a King dare not legally to do the like."[2] The kind of law they sought to protect their liberties as freemen, they believed, meant more than that; it meant also the existence of a regular order for the use of power.

It was not enough, moreover, to escape from the caprice of individuals or to take refuge in an inflexible code. The Puritans attempted to rest their governance upon the Bible; and eighteenth-century Americans turned with increasing frequency to what they knew of English common law. But these too proved inadequate to their demands — inconvenient in their restrictions and yet not far-reaching enough to guard the freedom they wished to protect.

Where there was no law, there was no freedom; and without a political order to secure adherence to those rules, liberty was conditional upon the whims of individuals. The purpose of law, in that sense, was not to abolish or restrain, but to preserve and enlarge freedom by providing predictable sanctions for the social order.[3]

The presumption that coercive power ought not to be used arbitrarily by individuals or self-constituted groups but ought rather to be exercised within defined procedures remained an American habit of thought. Exceptions were rarely tolerated and then only with much misgiving. Yet there are many puzzling aspects to the development and consequences of that presumption. For it was situated in a context of related views of who should participate in the use of force, of how authority was derived, of federalism, and of the media through which control was exercised.

The seventeenth-century colonists early confronted the necessity for decisions about the responsibility for the use of force. Almost from the start in New England, and elsewhere soon after the end of the garrison conditions of the first decades, they found traditional means of compulsion inadequate. The remoteness of the sovereign, the feebleness of transplanted institutions, and the pressure of the unsettling wilderness compelled anyone who wished to govern to enlist the collaboration of those over whom he intended to rule, lest he "sower their temper by contending with them in an indifferent matter." Force was manageable under these circumstances only when diluted with persuasion, as the prolonged controversies over representation in the assemblies and over the governors' salaries revealed. After the middle of the eighteenth century, Governor Hutchinson pointed out, no royal officer "would venture to take cognizance of any breach of law, against the general bent of the people."[4]

Thereafter there remained a connection between the willingness to accept the exercise of political power and the assurance that the subjects of control would participate in the decisions as to its use. The process by which that assurance developed has often been described with misleading simplicity in terms of the spread of democracy; it certainly stretches the meaning of the word so to refer to the pre-Revolutionary governments of America. Democracy was indeed the end result. But the process itself was complex and demands more precise analysis.

Who, for instance, was to take a part in making political decisions? The answer of Americans of the Revolutionary generation, based upon their practice of the preceding century, was that a broad inclusive category of persons, the citizens, were to do so. They thus gave the term quite a distinctive meaning, and one not clearly related to previous concepts.

The term, citizen, was not new in the 1770's; it had earlier been used by Greeks, Romans, and medieval Europeans, although not in the same way. Its primary meaning had been that of inhabitant of a city. On the other hand, the participants in the polity were the subjects of the king, a status related to allegiance; or they were denizens or inhabitants of a town or province, a status related to residence or the tenure of property. But the conception of citizenship as a general status, abstracted from such specific considerations and implying a share in political power, was novel.[5]

The idea did not emerge full-blown from the minds of the authors of the Declaration of Independence. They adopted it rather to describe the condition that a century and a half of development had brought into being in the colonies.

Americans had been left without a government through the effects of distance or of isolation or of the inappropriateness of transplanted forms. They had therefore been compelled to improvise one, and had learned to carry on that or any other public business with intelligence, order, and decision. A people capable of doing so had thereby become citizens.[6]

The implications of this conception of citizenship are still being explored. Almost at once it raised perplexing queries about existing assumptions with regard to the relation of the individual to the polity and with regard to the legitimacy and authority of government.

Citizenship was voluntary in nature. The founders of the Republic regarded the status as the product of an act of will of him who sought it. They provided for a regular procedure, naturalization, which brought with it all the rights of citizenship and was not dependent upon special acts as in England. Natives, of course, acquired citizenship by birth: but their case too involved an element of choice. They were presumed to make a decision to participate by remaining in the country; and the Indians who excluded themselves from the polity by their tribal organization were not reckoned citizens nor were those Americans who severed their native ties by permanent emigration.[7]

It followed from the view that citizenship was not entirely an incident of birth but also of choice, that the individual had a right to alter his status if he wished. That freemen could depart from the country had been maintained as far back as Magna Carta and affirmed in the Massachusetts Body of Liberties of 1641. That the subjects of foreign princes had the right to leave the lands of their birth was implicit in the American immigration policy; and the right of native Americans to depart from the United States was never challenged directly and, indirectly, only in the brief effort to use the passport for that purpose.[8]

The right of expatriation in America was corollary to that of migration. In Europe the subjects of a king were not considered to have dissolved their allegiance by departing from his realm. But in the New World, both before and after independence, immigrants were thought to have severed their old allegiances in leaving the countries of their birth; and they acquired new ones through naturalization. "Expatriation," declared an Act of 1868, "is a natural and inherent right of all people, indispensable to the enjoyment of the rights of life, liberty, and the pursuit of happiness; and . . . in recognition of this principle this Government has freely received emigrants from all nations, and invested them with the rights of citizenship." That position was maintained against Britain in the dispute over the impressment of seamen and later with regard to the right of asylum. Conversely, Americans through most of the nineteenth century attached no opprobrium to those who chose to transfer their loyalties elsewhere.[9]

By the same token, occasional exercise by the state of the power to deprive an individual of his citizenship also indirectly emphasized the voluntary rather than inherent character of that status. That the government should fix the terms of assent at naturalization or at any other time was consistent with the conception of participation in the polity as an act of will rather than as a condition of birth.[10]

The issue was not so clear when it came to the withdrawal or exclusion of whole communities. The right of secession, frequently argued before 1861, was decisively denied in the total crisis that began that year. But secession which destroyed all political procedures differed from the departure of an individual which left it intact.

The concept of citizenship as a condition involving participation in the polity created problems in a society which had usually associated power with status. The men of the revolutionary era could not simply divest themselves of inherited assumptions, and were forced to square the new with the old ideals by maintaining that all men could be citizens, but that some enjoyed less complete rights than others.

Suffrage and office-holding earlier had been privileges attached to property-holding status. These qualifications did not vanish immediately after 1776. But they could thereafter no longer be grounded on respect for privilege. Instead they were propped up by the argument that possession of property was a test of the fitness of the citizen to use power. That argument justified the exclusion of the propertyless from the ballot and from candidacy for office well into the nineteenth century. In time, the property qualification broke down under the pressure of new concepts of equality. But even while it survived it acquired a connotation that made it compatible with the idea of the citizen as a participant in the polity.[11]

The assumption that special training was a requisite for the proper exercise of citizenship later imposed analogous limitations upon the less educated, often with the ulterior motive of excluding Negroes or the foreign-born. The defense of a literacy requirement for voting rested upon the argument that such restrictions did not derogate from the rights of illiterates as citizens: they merely set up a test for fitness to exercise the suffrage.[12]

The concept of citizenship also made it necessary to explain the existence of large groups which were either excluded entirely from the category of citizens or only partially endowed with the rights attached to it. Slaves, Indians, aliens, free Negroes, and dependent persons such as women, children, and prisoners, were accorded limited rights as humans though not as citizens or else were denied any rights at all. Enlistment or conscription into the armed services also created special problems.

The existence of such underprivileged individuals had to be rendered compatible with the concept of citizenship. At the beginning of the seventeenth century, the places they occupied in the hierarchy of social status readily explained the fact that their privileges were less extensive than those of their superiors. The redefinition of citizenship as independent of status did not emancipate all these people; indeed, some like women and Negroes actually suffered a decline in the process. Thereafter Americans were compelled to justify the inferiority of such people in terms of their dependence as persons. They were not to be considered as a part of civil society either temporarily or permanently. The investigation of the rights of such groups has an intrinsic importance of its own and also will throw light on the situation of all Americans; for precedents of general validity have often been established in reference to them.[13]

The conception of citizenship was central in the definition of the participation of the individual in the exercise of power. The idea had been enunciated during the Revolution; but the practices on which it rested had already been developing for more than a century and a half and had by then raised important problems about the legitimacy of government and the nature of political authority.

Although both theory and practice in the United States identified the citizen as his own ruler, they allowed the individual or a group of individuals to use power on their own behalf only under exceptional circumstances. The ability to coerce could not be exercised autonomously; it had to be derived from an accepted source of authority.

This general assumption was involved in the intermittent concern for more than two centuries with the justification of revolution. The preoccupation with legitimacy helps to account for the fact that there have been no naked seizures of power in American history, hence no dictatorships and no practice of assassination. Therein lies a clear distinction from the recourse to violence in Latin American or Oriental governments.

When Americans took up arms in rebellion, for whatever cause, they grounded their actions in the right to resist the illegitimate use of power. They showed a significant concern with the preservation of proper procedures either by operating through existing governmental agencies or by quickly creating new ones. And, as in the case of Leisler and Shays, they accepted legitimate authority once it was clearly asserted. The Civil War created the problem it did because it involved, not a rebellion of individuals, but the action of recognized political entities, the Southern states, legitimately endowed with the power to govern.[14]

The issue was more clearly drawn during the American Revolution when the situation compelled men to argue, at the same time, in favor of legitimacy and rebellion. Those who embarked upon the course of resistance to royal authority in 1774 very shortly also had to concern themselves with the reconstruction of an effective political order. The perpetual revolutionaries like Tom Paine or Patrick Henry or John Randolph who did not move beyond questioning and criticism quickly found themselves out of tune with events. Most Americans considered rebellion a means not of destroying but of strengthening existing government. Their arguments and their thinking therefore were directed toward finding a conception of legitimacy that would simultaneously justify their disobedience to the Crown and establish the validity of the governments they were themselves forming.[15]

By the era of the Revolution legitimacy had come to have a meaning in the colonies different from the one it bore across the Atlantic. In Europe the dynasty of the monarch contained the line of legitimate political power well on into the nineteenth century. Neither Metternich nor his liberal and nationalistic opponents could conceive of a great state without at least the symbolic value of a crowned head. Yet, in the fifteen years of revolutionary debate after 1774, there was never a serious suggestion in America that kingship was a requisite of legitimate government. Instead, discussion and practice both reflected the assumption that legitimacy was a consequence not of royal assent but of the consent of the governed.

The ideas of the social compact and of the consent of the governed were by then familiar to European political theory;

these conceptions had long since been formulated in the writings of John Locke and in the experience of the revolution of 1688.[16] But in the Old World the monarch was still associated with the principles of contract and often was conceived as a party to it. He was not so regarded in the New World.

The explanation of the difference must lie in the development of a new conception of authority in eighteenth-century America. The first colonists had brought with them from Europe a conception of authority as hierarchically organized and descending from a single source, the sovereign monarch. That view subtly changed in succeeded generations, although it long survived across the Atlantic. The marks of the change were a growing habit of defiance or evasion of royal wishes, a steady loss of respect for the royal person and for the symbols of his majesty, and the disappearance of the charisma in which the throne had been enveloped. At the eve of the Revolution, the colonists could refer casually, without sense of lese majesty, to George III as a crowned ruffian; "the faith of king was now no more."[17]

By then Americans thought of authority not as descending downward from the throne, but as derived from below from the choices of the people. The consent of the governed referred not to an abstract compact between ruler and subject, as in the long tradition of European political theory, but to a process by which the people delegated power to their governors. Sometime in the century before the Revolution there must have been a change in the American view of the derivation of authority.[18]

We know too little as yet either about colonial political theory or political practice to account fully for that change. The dynamics of the process will no doubt emerge from more careful study of the ways in which power was exercised at the town or county level and of the relation of local to provincial government. But, whatever its origins, the conception of popular authority, like that of the citizen as a participant, established the basic procedures within which power was to be used in the United States.

The popular source of authority made possible the paradox of American federalism. In the United States the government consisted both of a congeries of sovereign states and also of a single sovereign state. The central and the state governments coexisted; all derived their powers from the consent of the people.

Federalism complicated the problems of procedure. The existence within certain areas of multiple jurisdictions affected men's views of the ways in which power was to be exercised.

In the past, the appeal to the principle of federalism has sometimes expressed discontent with the allocation of functions as between state and central government on the part of groups which expected more favorable treatment in one sphere than the other. Sometimes, however, that appeal has indirectly expressed a general reluctance to admit the validity of any form of government action at all. The opponents of economic regulation in the last quarter of the nineteenth century argued against the power of the state while that was the primary instrument of control. They shifted their objections to the national government when that began to act. Thus they attempted to create a shadowland of inactivity between the two jurisdictions by stressing the limitations on the power of whichever seemed most threatening at the moment. Federalism had the effect of erecting competing authorities which interested individuals or groups used as a means of defining procedure. But federalism was itself the product of a conception of authority in which two kinds of government coexisted, neither derived from the other but both grounded in popular consent.[19]

Since government derived its legitimacy from the consent of the citizen-participant, the channels for the expression of assent significantly influenced the procedures through which power was exercised. The central problem through most of American history was the extent to which the distribution of power within the polity accurately reflected popular authority.

By the time of the Revolution the principle most commonly recognized was that in a government organized in distinct and separate branches, the executive, legislative, and judicial would check and balance each other so that no one of them would exceed the capacity delegated to it. The separation of powers then had the support of a respectable body of political theory as well as of puissant examples from colonial experience.[20]

The concept of separation of powers, although the most explicitly formulated precisely because the phrases to describe it were available from widely read theorists, was only one aspect of the developing procedures of government. The founders of the American state were less concerned with preventing illegitimate actions than with furthering legitimate ones, that is, those which embodied the consent of the governed. It was therefore not merely necessary to separate the executive, the legislature, and the judiciary, but also to make each of them responsive to the people from whom their authority was derived. How that was effected is still by no means clear.

The institutional point of view which has dominated the study of the development of governmental forms has unbalanced the emphasis of the existing literature. There is abundant material on the evolution of the judiciary which occupies a central place in legal and constitutional history. Less attention has been paid to the process by which the modern chief executive, whether president or state governor, evolved out of his military, magisterial antecedent, the colonial governor. By the same token, a clearer insight into the seventeenth-century origins of the colonial assembly will contribute to an understanding of how that body became the modern legislature. Too often it has been assumed that these institutions were at the beginning what they became later.[21] The gaps in the available information make it difficult to discern the process by which the procedures for government, vested in these offices, became responsive to the will of the governed.

Common to these positions was the assumption that they were not to be held as occupations. Rotation or temporary tenure was the essence of Republicanism. "We may define a republic," the *Federalist* pointed out, as "a government which derives all its powers directly or indirectly from the great body of the people, and is administered by persons holding their offices during pleasure, for a limited period, or during good behavior."[22] The fixed term of office provided a mechanism by which the posts at which power was concentrated became vacant at predictable intervals. Their holders could therefore be displaced without impeachment, revolution, or assassination; and their prerogatives remained conditional upon the approval of those they ruled.

The idea of temporary tenure had not appeared until the eighteenth century and it emerged out of peculiar conditions. Political offices in seventeenth-century Europe were held under a variety of tenures. Some, feudal in origins, descended by inheritance. Others came by purchase as a species of property. Still others, representative in character, like membership in the House of Commons, were held for the life of the body. And, finally, those which came as grants through royal commission were valid indefinitely at the king's pleasure.[23]

The colonies followed these usages with regard to a limited range of officers, primarily those which were closely linked to the Crown. Another model was available however. In English municipal, joint-stock, and other corporations, the members annually selected their officers; and it was this model the colonies emulated as far as royal restrictions permitted them to. In the eighteenth century the practice of annual election spread and acquired the intellectual support of Greek and Roman precedents. It entered almost automatically into the framing of the state and federal constitutions. It did not always involve the unqualified choice of the recipient of the largest number of votes; such considerations as seniority were also important.[24]

The emphasis on periodic elections was closely linked to the evolving conception of proper procedure. The fact that many colonies actually originated in joint-stock companies, of course, supplied an institutional connection to their practices. But, in addition, the slowly developing view of what public office was, demanded such elections.

In the eighteenth century, an election rarely presented the voters with a genuine choice of candidates. The governors of Connecticut and Rhode Island and the members of all the Assemblies held their seats year after year, often without contest. Nevertheless, annual election was important as a means by which the populace assented to the grant of power. Even if it had no more than a ritual significance, the requirement for annual election recognized that the individual officeholder had no inherent claim upon the office and held it upon sufferance as a trust.

That was why proprietary or feudal forms of tenure were not successfully transplanted to the colonies. The practical conditions of the society made such appointments valueless in the absence of popular consent.[25]

It followed from these assumptions, too, that no test of competence was a prerequisite. The sole qualification of the officeholder was his ability to command the consent of those over whom he held power. In practice, only a single individual or a very few enjoyed that ability. The process of choice was none the less meaningful.

The active participation of the citizen in the designation

of his officials in America added a totally new dimension to the conception of the consent of the governed. Consent was not simply the abstract product of a theoretical compact with a ruler but rather a concrete procedure for the actual use of power.

By the time of the Revolution, the conceptions of citizenship, of authority, and of public office established procedures by which government could use force, with authority derived from the consent of the governed and exercised temporarily by individuals drawn from among the body of the people. The safeguards of liberty lay not in the denial of the use of force, but in the establishment of appropriate procedures for its use.

These procedures, even when formalized in written constitutions, changed in response to shifts in the political and social forces that operated on them after the last two decades of the eighteenth century. The most important developments came in the relations of the holders of office to the people from whom they derived their power.

So long as only one candidate stood for office or so long as a single individual or a family retained a presumptive claim year after year, the voter could, in effect, do no more than say yea or nay; and that limited the extent to which his consent influenced the power used in his name. When the elective process was slowly transformed from a device for securing assent to one in which the transfer of power became a genuine possibility, the elector acquired the capacity for shaping the alternatives presented to him.

Conceivably, elections under the Republic might have continued as earlier simply to ratify the choices of powerful or eminent individuals or cliques. Or, conceivably, the state-founding groups might have institutionalized their control over the process of designation, as did the Congress in India, Mapai in Israel, and Neo-Destour in Tunis.[26] Developments in the United States followed quite a different course — one which extended rather than restricted the importance of the voter's consent.

The American elector acquired the capacity for effective choice because the colonies had begun to devise nomination machinery in the eighteenth century. The experiments by the Connecticut and Rhode Island Assemblies with procedures for electing their governors, the caucus in Boston, and the activities of the Sons of Liberty, were early efforts to bring alternative candidates before the electorate.[27] The Revolutionary generation was disposed to identify such efforts with the disruptive factions and selfish cabals blamed for the failings of the House of Commons. The safety of the Republic seemed to lie in its ability to dissolve such groups through a representative system that would assure the election of preeminent individuals who could balance the competing interests in the society.[28] As a result neither the federal nor the original state constitutions made any explicit provision for nomination.

The party system later remedied that deficiency by supplying a mechanism for the designation of candidates that was responsive to popular consent and that united groups dispersed over considerable areas. For the first half-century of the Republic the parties were essentially local organizations, but an intricate development then gave them national form. In the twentieth century, they became integrated into the established election procedures as the government assumed oversight over their place in the primaries and even over their internal operations. Although the more recent adjustments to the growing size of the electorate and to the new media of communications have complicated the nature of the citizen's assent, the creation of procedures for nomination has widened the range of choices available to him and has extended the significance of his consent to be governed.[29]

Another category of offices has emerged since the ratification of the Constitution. The expansion of governmental services created places held permanently as occupations, and therefore related to power and to popular consent in quite a different way from those which were elected and terminal. It is difficult to discuss these developments simply because of certain ambiguities in American terminology. Yet they are extremely important in the evolution of political procedures.

In the latter part of the eighteenth century, the term "police" was used in two senses when it was not conflated with "polity" or "policy." It referred in the first instance to a governmental function, that of regulation in the interest of health and security. This was the earlier meaning and it comprehended all the activities of the community. To police a city was to maintain order, cleanliness, and decency; it included oversight over wells, sewerage, disease, and garbage disposal as well as the apprehension of criminals. The rapidly growing municipalities of the New World regarded these tasks as important and devoted a good deal of attention to them.[30]

The word, police, also referred to a hired body of officers endowed with power to enforce the law — the sense in which the term now survives. By the eighteenth century, such officers had already appeared and played an important role on the continent of Europe.

While Americans regarded the function as important, they viewed the mercenaries with disfavor; and they never acquired the respect for the cops that the English did for the Bobbies. The revolutionary experience persuaded the free citizens of the United States that a police force, in the second sense, was a threat to republican institutions. "The business of police," wrote William Tudor in 1809, "is fortunately incompatible with the nature of our government, and is always clumsily and ineffectually managed; individuals succeed better, and do not endanger constitutional principles." Policing *functions* were to be confined to citizens elected for the purpose — watch and ward, sheriffs and their posses, constables, marshals, and overseers of various types. In the United States, through the first third of the nineteenth century, individuals who wished greater protection than was thus afforded were expected to provide it themselves through hired watchmen and the like. Even general problems, like juvenile delinquency or the dangers from fire, were handled through voluntary civic organizations. Any large-scale riot or disorder led to a call for the citizens' militia.[31]

It is a problem of immense importance to trace the development, and the effects upon liberty, of professional officers endowed with policing powers. No serious effort has yet been made to do so.

Municipal police forces began to appear in the 1840's. Central organizations were set up in New York City in 1844, in Chicago in 1851, in New Orleans in 1852, and in Boston in 1854. These were only rudimentary. Often their administrative heads were elected; and their members occupied a menial status, reflected in their refusal to wear uniforms by which they might be identified. They were poorly organized public watchmen of a sort, still charged with such duties as oversight of the streets and lamps. The growth of cities made the problem more urgent, and the opportunities for violence during the Civil War created a crisis. Only then did systematic organization of municipal police forces enter its modern phase.[32]

The states were content for even longer with what power a citizens' militia gave them. The earliest state police forces appeared in the 1880's, in response to the demand for an instrument of power not locally or popularly controlled. The First World War gave a significant impetus to the movement, when the states lost their only source of organized power with the entry of their militias into military service as the national guard. New York and Michigan created their troops in 1917; and the spread of criminality beyond the limits of

the city with the wide use of the automobile further stimulated the trend.[33]

The earliest federal police agency was in the Customs
Service; and as the Treasury grew in importance with the
rise of federal expenditures and the expansion of internal
and external revenues, the police powers of the Department
also grew. At the end of the nineteenth century, other
branches of the government which needed similar services
had to borrow agents from the Treasury or hire private
detectives like the Pinkertons. Only the Post Office had a
similar, though smaller, body of investigators.

In 1908, Congress refused to authorize the Justice Department to create a Bureau of Investigation. "It would be a
great blow to freedom and to free institutions if there should
arise in this country any such great central secret-service
bureau as there is in Russia," explained Congressman Waldo
of New York. Nevertheless, President Theodore Roosevelt,
in defiance of the wishes of Congress, allowed Attorney
General Bonaparte to set up the bureau which at first dealt
primarily with crimes on government reservations and in the
District of Columbia. The jurisdiction of the F.B.I. expanded
rapidly with the enactment of the Mann Act in 1910, with
vast wartime assignments, with the application of the commerce clause to crime, and with the later problems of dis-
loyalty.[34]

The concern of the framers of the Constitution with the
subordination of military to civil authority led the United
States to rely almost entirely on citizen soldiers for national
defense. A professional federal army of any size did not
emerge until recently and has rarely been used within the
country's frontiers.[35]

The emergence of professional police forces was a significant aspect of the development of a still more widespread
bureaucracy. The whole trend raised serious questions about
the assumption that liberty could be safeguarded only by

procedures for the use of power entrusted to temporary agents of the people.

The more general challenge to the principle of rotation in office had earlier arisen out of the desire to protect the independence of the judiciary. The assurance of tenure during good behavior for the federal, and for some of the state judges did not at first set these officeholders off from any others. In the 1790's judicial and administrative posts were regarded in much the same way, except that the former had no limit of term. But, after 1800, the experience of the federal bench under John Marshall gave support to the conception of the judge as a nonpolitical arbiter.[36]

That role drew attention to the fact that the occupants of the bench were largely chosen by the executive or the legislature rather than directly by the people. If the judiciary were also secure in office for life and unresponsive to popular wishes, the connection between their actions and the consent of the governed all but disappeared.

The response was a demand, growing louder through the nineteenth century, for application of the elective, terminal principle to judges. The claim to a-political character seemed inconsistent with the fact that judges were still able concurrently to hold other positions and to become candidates for office. As a result, in time the benches of almost all the states were filled by the ballot. After 1900 resentment at the autonomy of the courts led also to the call for popular review of judicial decisions.[37]

These efforts did not prevail for they ran counter to a more powerful current that confirmed the independence of the judiciary. Toward the end of the nineteenth century, the state judges began to vest themselves in distinctive robes to emphasize their impartial, almost sacerdotal role and to thwart the tendency toward greater responsiveness to the people. The growing complexity of the law and the organization of the legal profession provided a foundation for the argument that special preparation was necessary to a judicial career, and that the ballot box was not an effective means for selecting judges. A variety of devices then appeared for circumventing popular choices in many states so that only men qualified by the standards of the profession would mount to the bench.[38]

In the latter half of the nineteenth century the argument for expertness in the judiciary was applied to other offices. The number of clerks and technicians in the agencies of government grew steadily; and some of them acquired regulative functions. The bureaucrats were at first without power; their task was primarily to collect information, not to take the initiative in enforcement. But the distinction was difficult to maintain; and in time, these officials acquired the power to act, along with staffs of inspectors armed with quasi-police powers. Later still some agencies acquired quasi-judicial powers.[39]

The growth of a vast army of bureaucrats created an immediate problem of control. In Europe, the transition from earlier systems to that of civil service by some measure of ability was fairly easy. But in the United States, republican assumptions about the need for rotation of offices among the citizens without regard to qualifications complicated the transition. Nevertheless, the staggering problems of disposing of the patronage as the administrative cadres grew larger, and the desire for greater efficiency, led to a gradual alteration in American practice.[40]

The adjustment in the United States did not take the simple form the dedicated civil service reformers of the 1880's anticipated. A substantial number of jobs remained in the patronage pool available to the party in power. Other posts, particularly at the upper levels of the Foreign Service and the regulatory agencies, were declared nonpartisan or extra-political, to be filled by qualified experts. And a great mass of places were thrown open to impersonal competition by examinations of one sort or another. All remained responsible, in theory at least, to an elected official. But, to the extent that the bureaucrats acquired extended tenure and independence from political pressure, they also widened the distance between themselves and the people with whose consent they were presumed to govern.

In theory, each official was linked in a chain of responsibility that led through his superior to the President or governor and thus to the people. In practice, the chain could hardly transmit a firm sense of accountability; the local postal clerk was conscious of the postmaster, but rarely of the Postmaster General or the President and more rarely still of the people he served. Public information about the affairs of an agency through formal regular reports or through informal exposure occasionally restored the sense of responsibility; but agencies all too soon learned to protect themselves either by carefully guarding the information they released or by shrouding their affairs in secrecy. More generally, the citizen had few clues as to where to look in the complex apparatus of government for the activities to which he was presumed to consent.

The prolonged concern in the United States with the methods of appointment reflected the hesitation to permit the accumulation of power outside the procedures which embodied consent. The reluctance to permit elected officials to delegate their powers to appointed ones and the fear of personal as against impersonal or law-regulated actions also contributed to the disquiet of many citizens as the machinery of government grew more elaborate.

The evolution of a corpus of administrative law, systematized in the Administrative Procedure Act of 1946, showed some preoccupation with the need for preserving in other forms the standards of proper process. The development of the bureaucracy, like the development of professional police forces, raised difficult questions with regard to the location of power. For the ability to apply compulsion through procedures which did not directly reflect the consent of the governed certainly affected the liberty of those coerced. The extent to which it did and the countervailing gains for those on whose behalf it was done must be measured in order to estimate the social effects.

The evidence from the history of the United States is by no means clear as to whether the consequences of bureaucratization have unfolded along the lines predicted by such theorists as Max Weber. It seems safer to follow Mill in the premise that "no absolute rule can be laid down," and that a sound judgment of the impact on liberty will only emerge from an examination in detail of how the bureaucracy operated.[41] Unfortunately, an adequate basis for such conclusions is still lacking.

With regard to all these developments, the answers to the following questions are unclear. What personal motives and social expectations produced the professional officeholders? What was the character of the opposition to them? What powers did they acquire, explicitly by grant, implicitly by usage? What was their effect upon earlier procedures? At what point and to what extent did they acquire a monopoly of the use of power? What has been their effect upon individual rights?

Only the answers to these questions will make it possible to assess the extent to which the developments of the past century have altered the capacity of the citizens to consent to their government, and thus to legitimatize the procedures through which political power is exercised. From such an assessment it will be possible to judge whether, despite changes in specific procedures, the concept of proper procedures remained intact.

The obligation to work within the existing rules has always been irksome. To the extent that procedures became better defined, the opportunities for tight control of them widened. Individuals and groups dissatisfied with their share of control then sought their own advantage by devising modes of action to by-pass the accepted procedures. Even those who held power under the pressure of a crisis were sometimes tempted to dispense with restraining forms.

The effort to circumvent constitutional limitations was an important element in the evolution of political parties until those acquired a place, recognized by law, in the procedures of the polity. More recently a variety of pressure groups have often influenced decisions outside the formal framework of government. The lobbies of the last quarter of the nineteenth century and the vast array of organizations representing economic, ethnic, and religious interests that emerged after 1900 have played a significant role in shaping legislation. They have also offered an approach to power to those who considered themselves inadequately represented. Participation in such activities was itself a preparation for politics and gave many men and women access to the ranks of the politically active. From that point of view these nongovernmental instrumentalities have operated to widen the area of assent, and they have time and again dissolved the feelings of frustration that, under other conditions, have turned men in total opposition to intractably rigid political procedures.[42]

The possibility of evading the rules has had dangerous consequences. On exceptional occasions the desire for quick results has led to a waiver of proper procedures. The emergencies of the Civil War and the two world wars are the best-known examples. Vigilante activity in many parts of the country and at many periods also sprang from the same impulse. At another level, the debate over courts of equity reflected a significant concern with the propriety of escaping from the rigid rules of procedure that normally encompassed the exercise of power.

In some of these cases the lapses were temporary. As significant as the reactions to the emergencies of war was the ability to restore normality with the coming of peace. The fears expressed during crises for the fate of civil liberties often sprang from an underestimation of the resiliency of the procedures evaded for the moment.

In other cases, as in the development of political parties, the devices for evasion in time became a part of the structure of accepted procedures. Still others, like the pressure groups, remained outside the formal apparatus of government although vaguely recognized by it.

The history of these evolving relationships will throw a good deal of light upon the conditions of freedom in the United States. What is crucial in each instance is not whether the procedures were susceptible to modification, but whether the change or the lack of change made the use of political power more or less responsive to the consent of the governed.

The confinement of force within rules of procedure has had a direct effect upon the liberties of Americans. The process of securing consent was itself a mechanism for the accommodation of differences; and necessities accepted by free choice blurred the abstract distinction between compulsion and permissiveness.[43]

The political leaders who operated within these procedures were not theoretical philosophers and rarely expressed explicitly the rules they took for granted. But, embedded in their use of the term Union are connotations which spring out of the assumption that the procedures for consent are central to the American polity. When Madison or Lincoln spoke of Union they had in mind not simply the antithesis of secession. Secession in their view was the "essence of anarchy"; it did violence to the idea of Union by rupturing the complex of rules, arrived at by consent, that permitted the use of power to extend men's liberties.[44]

For many Americans the conviction that the rules were the

product of their own consent gave a high degree of predictability to the incidence of force in the society. Their liberty was bound in with the orderly application of power in a manner which protected men through restraints they themselves accepted. They were able to control their lives with the assurance that the compulsions that operated on them were the products of their own wills and subject to limitations that they could themselves impose.

☆ III ☆
THE LIMITS
OF
POLITICAL
POWER

THE Americans created a polity by defining the procedures for the use of coercive power. In the continuing process of doing so they fully expected that the state which was the product of their own consent would extend rather than contract their freedom.

They were therefore ever alive to the danger that the rulers might misuse their power. Knowledge of history and of the contemporary experience of Europe made the citizens of the Republic vividly conscious of the propensity of force to intoxicate those to whom it was entrusted. The governmental procedures evolved in the United States consequently contained devices to inhibit the capacity to act of the individuals entrusted with power and also to guarantee their dependence upon the consent of the governed whose agents they were.

Yet the formal mechanism alone did not assure restraint in the use of the state's coercive machinery. In crises, genuine or imagined, it was always possible to evade procedural checks; and the facility of doing so frequently justified the fear that the government might turn into an engine for destroying rather than for furthering the liberty of the people.

These anxieties reflected a conviction that, altogether apart from purely procedural restraints, there were absolute limits beyond which the state ought never to use coercion. Liberty depended not only upon the use of compulsive power within appropriate procedures but also upon confining it within recognized bounds. To describe the development of freedom in the United States it is necessary therefore to examine the forces that shaped the limits to government action.

The problem of absolute limits was rarely discussed explicitly, for the tactics of political debate usually obscured the abstract question. It was easier to arrive at acceptable decisions by discussing the propriety of a specific measure, or the competence of a particular officer or agency than by raising general issues. Above all, those threatened by the adverse effects of action were more likely to seek refuge in procedural defenses than in appeals to general principle.

An examination of how Americans sought to prevent government at any level from operating where they thought it ought not reveals a tenacious insistence that there were limits to its competence. Federalism and constitutionalism supplied the most important formal impediments to the unbounded use of political power. The description of the terms of government in a written document which dispersed sovereignty among several entities rather than concentrated it in one of them, determined how power would be exercised. But, by opening the possibility of appeals either to the constitutions or to rival jurisdictions, it indirectly provided the means of attenuating any powers considered improper or disadvantageous. In addition to these procedural restraints upon the state's ability to act there was an underlying assumption that in some matters it ought not to take action at all.

After 1789, the existence in the United States of multiple governmental jurisdictions, set off from one another by only vague lines of demarcation, set bounds around the powers of both the states and the nation. Interested parties who wished to immobilize the government or to seek favorable treatment from it often preferred to play one jurisdiction off against another rather than to depend upon abstract principle for a judgment of the merits of their case. The very useful material in the extensive historical and legal literature on federalism has dealt largely with the constitutional issues so raised.[1]

Federalism however has exerted a wider influence upon the scope of political power than these formulations of the problem suggest. For federalism itself rested upon the assumption that multiple focuses of power were inherently desirable as safeguards to the liberties of the citizens. That assumption antedated the appearance of a formal federal system, and made possible the appeals to states' rights or to national authority as impediments to undesirable actions.

Traces of this assumption were evident in the seventeenth century. The coexistence of several contiguous, yet autonomous, colonies in practice limited the powers of each by creating avenues of escape from their jurisdictions. The open borders of Rhode Island and Virginia were an invitation to dissidents who wished to evade the rulings of the magistrates of Massachusetts or of the proprietor of Maryland.[2]

Furthermore, the rapid devolution of power from the central provincial governments had somewhat the same result. The weakness of the lines of command and the inability to apply power in many districts without the collaboration of the men on the spot endowed local units of government with practical autonomy. Governors and assemblies learned that their wishes could be frustrated by an intractable town or parish and that limited their capacity to act. Indeed, the growing power of the towns and other localities gave some colonies a quasi-federal structure and had a significant influence upon the conception of authority itself. Often the assemblies acted less like continuing legislative bodies than like congresses composed of delegates from autonomous governing entities.[3]

At the other end of the political spectrum, occasional efforts to develop supracolonial institutions sometimes appeared to set limits upon the individual colonies. The Confederation and the Dominion of New England and the various plans of union devised between 1750 and 1774 experimented with ways of circumscribing the power of the provinces by creating some more comprehensive political unit.[4]

The Founders of the Republic were thoroughly familiar with the practice of allocating power to plural jurisdictions rather than to a unitary one. When they considered the historical experience of earlier confederacies, one flaw seemed invariably to have led either to anarchy or to tyranny. From the Amphictyonic League to the United Netherlands, these were hierarchic arrangements of states; and "a sovereignty over sovereigns, a government over governments, a legislation for communities, as contradistinguished from individuals, as it is a solecism in theory, so in practice it is subversive of the order and ends of civil polity."[5] Both the Articles of Confederation and the Constitution provided, although in differing degrees, for a union not merely of states but of people. After the adoption of the Constitution each of the governing entities, operating within its own orbit, dealt directly, and not merely through intermediaries, with the citizens.

The revolutionary generation was able to arrive at this solution because it conceived of authority as emanating from the consent of the governed rather than as descending from a single sovereign and because practice had shown that governors and selectmen, J.P.'s and vestrymen, acting in their own spheres, provided desirable counterpoises to one another. While then and later there were significant differences in points of view as to how much power should be assigned to the national as against the state governments, there was no dissent over the fundamental federal structure; and there was virtually unanimous agreement that that structure would itself safeguard liberty by setting limits upon the scope of action of every agency within it. The conception of limits was not a product of federal procedures, but rather a justification for them already in existence by the time they were formally incorporated in the Constitution.[6]

Consequently, the Constitution did not permanently fix the relations of the various political entities to each other. Later efforts to contract or expand the limits of government action continued to shift the lines between federal and state jurisdictions. But the idea of multiple jurisdictions remained intact. Between 1865 and 1900 the power of the national government increased steadily. The more frequent recourse to the federal judiciary and the emergence of such agencies as the Interstate Commerce Commission were products not merely of the desire of some to broaden the powers of the central government, but also of efforts of others to use it as an impediment to state action. This tendency was evident in the field of social welfare and also in regard to economic policy.[7]

However, the ascendancy of the federal over the state governments by no means became total. Various groups have sought the protection of state law against the consequences of federal policy. States from time to time have used personal liberty, alien land, segregation, and right-to-work laws in an effort to frustrate or evade federal fugitive slave, immigration, civil rights, and labor policies. Similarly, the resistance of the producing states prevented the adoption of a federal oil conservation program and limited control over the industry to an interstate compact.[8]

Furthermore, the states have by no means extirpated the

autonomy of the political entities within them. School boards and municipalities usually lacked constitutional guarantees of their integrity; yet they often retained a *de facto* capacity for action, derived from the support of their citizens rather than from the legislature; and they were significantly strengthened by the home-rule movements of the past century. Despite all the contemporary tendencies toward centralization, local government held on to an ability to experiment that reflected a persistent looseness in political organization. As a result, even centrally sponsored activities were often administered through autonomous local agencies in the belief that power could thus be more safely disposed.[9]

Federalism has been more than a fortuitous arrangement or the product of the historical circumstances of colonial settlement. The limits it has imposed on government action have not been entirely procedural. The existence of multiple governmental jurisdictions has rather reflected the assumption that such limits upon all agencies were themselves desirable; and federalism has offered a convenient instrument for effectively maintaining restraints upon the use of coercive power.

The American concept of constitutionalism embodied an analogous concern with establishing restraints upon the power of government. Procedural limits are inherent in the idea of a written document that defines the structure of the polity. In addition Americans have appealed to constitutions to establish absolute limits on the capacity of the state to act.

Already in the seventeenth century, aggrieved settlers were inclined to turn to their charters for novel definitions of authority, claiming, for instance, that those grants from the Crown confined its power in ways it could not itself alter. In some provinces the Puritan idea of covenant sustained that argument; the King, like God, of his own will accepted rules to govern the use of his sovereign powers, and could not act outside those rules. So, too, under frontier conditions men, compelled to improvise the agencies by which they would be governed, often entered upon compacts that were in the nature of constitutional documents, which described what the polity could and could not do. Implicit in all these formulations was the tenacious assumption, which lacked legal support, that such compacts were irrevocable and unalterable.[10]

As a result, by the time the states confronted the task of devising their own constitutions in the 1770's, Americans had ceased to think of them as Englishmen did. In the New World the term, constitution, no longer referred to the actual organization of power developed through custom, prescription, and precedent. Instead it had come to mean a written frame of government setting fixed limits on the use of power. The American view was, of course, closely related to the rejection of the old conception that authority descended from the Crown to its officials. In the newer view — that authority was derived from the consent of the governed — the written constitution became the instrument by which the people entrusted power to their agents.[11]

Appeals to constitutions as limits upon governmental action grew more frequent after 1780 and still more so after 1789. The bitter controversies that led to the Civil War did not weaken the respect for constitutionalism; the Confederacy, in that regard, followed the precedent of the Republic. But such appeals after 1780 were more usually tied to specific provisions within the documents than earlier; and it became increasingly difficult to make out whether the appeals dealt with matters of procedure or with limits absolutely and abstractly conceived. A good deal of the nineteenth-century discussion of such problems as the separation of powers, the process of judicial review, and the concept of checks and balances hinged upon that question.[12]

The growing concern with constitutionalism as a limit upon government action was supported by an accretion of interests concerned with minimizing the role of the State. But always it remained tactically more effective to oppose government action by reference to procedural rather than substantive limits. The techniques of political debate and of legal disputation tended to obscure the distinction.

There had always been a profound ambiguity to the American position. The colonists had argued that objectionable measures, such as internal taxes levied by Parliament, were inconsistent with the "fundamental principles of the English constitution," and contrary to "our charters, the express conditions on which our progenitors relinquished their native countries." This legalistic approach could not consistently be maintained, for that would have rested their defense upon uncertain interpretations of the intent of the original grants and upon the doubtful proposition that the charters were not subject to revocation or alteration. As a result the Americans had been compelled to appeal also to "the clear voice of natural justice" which showed that the offensive laws were "contradictory to the law of nature." In doing so, they had assumed that there were absolute limits upon the power of the Crown, apart from those spelled out in the charters.[13]

The adoption of a written constitution did not resolve this ambiguity. Frequent appeals in the nineteenth century to the long-held conceptions of natural law and natural justice revealed the persistence of the conviction that limits to the use of power did not depend entirely upon written texts. Constitutionalism did not create those limits, but was a useful instrument for making them effective.[14]

At the middle of the nineteenth century, occasional attacks upon the conception of constitutionalism began to emerge as a consequence of the ambiguity about whether the limits upon government derived from the written text or from an antecedent body of unwritten natural law. If the latter were the case, then aggrieved men could appeal to a higher authority against the Constitution; they could demand that the government not do even that which the fundamental charter permitted. Thus, William Lloyd Garrison denounced the Constitution as "a covenant with death and an agreement with Hell" because it recognized the legality of slavery. He was not aware that, in doing so, he stood at the head of a line of thinkers who denied totally the basic presumption that any limit to government action existed. For, if the higher law forbade measures that the Constitution permitted, it also enjoined or commanded such as the Constitution forbade. Power could be used in any way the individual conscience interpreted natural law, a conviction that converted the pacifist into a belligerent supporter of the Civil War. Such criticism formed an important strain in later progressive thought; and it helped to align some of the extreme populists in an assault upon the whole social order. In the first decades of the twentieth century it contributed to the interpretation of the Constitution as a class instrument imposed on the nation by fraud.[15]

This point of view always remained that of a minority, whose exuberant rhetoric and professions of disinterested advocacy of the people obscured its limited following. That constitutionalism maintained a strong hold on American opinion was revealed in the reaction to the New Deal court packing plan in 1937. Altogether apart from the merits of the plan and from its actual constitutionality, the incident, coming as it did at the high tide of progressive influence, revealed widespread determination to maintain some limits on the power even of an enormously popular government. Whatever the political maneuvers that shaped the outcome of the contest, an impressive number of sincere supporters of the New Deal turned against it on this issue.

The lawyers and the other foes of the New Deal who

fought the scheme had been decisively defeated at the polls only a year earlier. Nevertheless they were able to summon up a body of support much broader than they imagined existed. The Supreme Court was then in low repute after a succession of decisions that were generally resented as arbitrary and narrow. It was out of no desire to protect the Court's prerogatives that opposition to the plan snowballed, but rather out of a conviction that there ought to be no tampering with the fundamental constitutional arrangements. The intellectual and emotional presuppositions drawn into the controversy reveal the extent to which the constitution was regarded as the procedural instrument for maintaining absolute limits on the power of the state.[16]

American experience with both federalism and constitutionalism demonstrated that beyond the purely procedural restraints there were absolute limits to state action. The citizens of the Republic and their colonial predecessors did not view the problem in formal terms; they did not concede to the state the power to act whenever procedures were available for doing so. Instead they were always conscious that there were some actions the government ought not to take and sought procedural grounds in federalism and constitutionalism to inhibit it.

The line between what was permissible and what was not was conventionally described as that between the power of the state and the rights of the individual. In 1641, the Massachusetts Body of Liberties had collected and expressed "such liberties immunities and privileges as humanity, civility and Christianity call for as due every man in his place and proportion"; and gave assurance that those rights would be "inviolably enjoyed" forever.[17] The natural-rights philosophy, particularly in the form expressed by John Locke, supplied a theoretical foundation and a descriptive vocabulary for the belief Americans already held that neither the government nor any other agency could trespass upon the freedom of action the citizen reserved to himself with regard to certain matters. The Declaration of Independence spoke, as a matter of course, of life, liberty, and the pursuit of happiness as among the natural and unalienable rights of man. The Virginia and Massachusetts constitutions set up formal provisions to prevent infringement upon some of those rights, as did the first ten amendments to the Federal Constitution.[18] By the middle of the nineteenth century Americans commonly thought of their rights as a solid barrier that could be readily defined in handbooks and that covered everything from the most general constitutional provisions to the details of business negotiations.[19] Only the reaction of Southern intellectuals in the defense of slavery raised genuine questions as to the validity of those rights; and their arguments did not take hold even in their own section, except as racism offered a basis for treating Negroes as an excluded category.[20]

The source and nature of those rights was by no means clear. American conditions which tended to destroy inherited institutions, habits, and customs generated frequent claims that the individual was himself competent to guide his own conduct and gave him the presumptive right to do so. The definition of rights therefore proceeded not through the logical development of theory but in response to evolving practices. Rights which were never invaded, never received explicit formulation; men simply acted as if they existed. In other cases, the assertion of a right came in resistance to some challenge to it and was expressed in negative terms. The resistance to the challenge was itself evidence that a positive belief in the right had already developed. Whence? Still other rights were widely respected long before they were explicitly recognized in legal or constitutional documents and sometimes despite the fact they were never so recognized at all.

That was why a different and wider conception of rights prevailed in the colonies for a half-century before independence than was recognized in England. In 1735, for example, Andrew Hamilton argued successfully that the only valid restraint upon the natural right of a printer to complain or remonstrate against public officials was the truth or falsity of his statements. He could point to no statute or precedent in English law by way of justification, yet his stand won widespread approval and was later embodied in the American conception of freedom of the press.[21]

Similarly, the traditional limitations upon the freedom of movement broke down at the end of the seventeenth century without formal action. The right of settlement was *de facto* established, and thereafter occasional efforts by states or municipalities to select their residents have rarely been effective. Freedom to travel was unchallenged although sustained by no explicit guarantees.[22] The conception of privacy as a right also seems independent of explicit formulation; it was respected in advance of any direct protection from statutes or binding judicial decisions.[23] Squatters were conceded to have a kind of property right long before the law formally recognized it.[24] There has been a widespread belief in the right to freedom of scientific inquiry and of teaching, even in the absence of constitutional bars to interference.[25] There has been a quiet but decisive acquiescence in the right of men and women to choose their own partners in marriage, to decide on the number of, and the character of, the upbringing of their children, to select their own occupations, and, in general, to regulate their family life without external restraint.[26]

All such rights by the early eighteenth century were not considered dependent upon a grant from any source, nor conditioned on any status in society, but inherent in the nature of man. If they were described in a document, it was only by way of confirmation. The rights themselves were anterior to any explicit recording of them.

There is therefore more validity than has been usually accorded to the contention of the defenders of the Federal Constitution in 1787 and 1788 that a Bill of Rights was superfluous. In England, James Wilson explained, liberties were derived "from the gift and grant of the King, and no wonder the people were anxious to obtain bills of rights; but here the fee simple remains in the people." Any powers they did not explicitly delegate to the government, remained their own. Their rights were absolute and the specifying of them could do no more than provide forms for their defense. Indeed, the definition of a right might actually narrow it by the implication that that which was omitted was excluded. For that reason the Ninth Amendment provided that, "The enumeration in the Constitution of certain rights, shall not be construed to deny or disparage others retained by the people."[27]

Consequently, it was never possible to develop a reasoned catalogue of what the rights of men were. It is true that the political theorists, particularly those inspired by Locke, wrote as if that task were feasible. They distinguished natural from civil rights, those already in existence in the state of nature and those dependent upon membership in society. The former involved the interests of no person but the individual and were therefore absolute; the latter affected other men and were therefore subject to control by the government. Every effort to apply this distinction to concrete matters encountered insuperable difficulties. John Stuart Mill, for example, had to argue that prohibition and Sabbath-observance laws offended individual rights, but that control by the state of family size did not.[28]

Significantly, few Americans even attempted to spell out the distinction between natural and civil rights, although many accepted it in theory. Instead they were content with either vague general affirmations as in the Declaration of Independence or with specific negatives upon such forms of state action that seemed immediately dangerous, as in the first ten amendments.

The Bills of Rights attached to the federal and some state constitutions were in the character of enumerations of actions the government might not take. But they made no effort to present a reasoned or comprehensive listing. The items included were thrown together haphazardly and somewhat capriciously as if in the nature of illustrations rather than of an exhaustive catalogue.[29]

Nor were these enumerations interpreted with any degree of consistency. Even the rights embodied in constitutional impediments to government action, such as those contained in the First and Fourteenth amendments, have not been frozen in any fixed form. They have rather developed in the past two centuries, in accord with changes — which were not purely legal in character — in the view of what the limits of the use of force should be. There was a long way to go, for instance, between the First Amendment's interdiction of a religious establishment by the federal government and the Supreme Court's affirmation in 1872, that "the law knows no heresy and is committed to the support of no dogma," because "the full and free right to entertain any religious belief" was conceded to all. Shifts in the connotation of that right continue to the very present.[30]

Under the pressure of social conditions, most clearly enunciated rights have been forgotten or obscured, or else their intent has totally been transformed — often without serious objection. Without protest or controversy, local laws have effectively contravened "the right of the people to keep and bear Arms" guaranteed by the Second Amendment to the federal constitution. More vaguely stated provisions like the assurance of the assistance of counsel and of trial "by an impartial jury" in the Sixth Amendment have necessarily been subject to continuing interpretation.[31]

By the same token, property rights were susceptible to

wide-ranging variations in judgment. In the post-revolutionary period, Americans who sought a liberal patent system to encourage manufacturing took it as a matter of course that such security was one of the natural rights of all men, there being no property more peculiarly a man's own than that which was produced by the labor of his mind. A century later analogous redefinitions of property rights for a time gave employers and employees the freedom to contract at will, unhampered by legislative regulations.

On the other hand, the nineteenth-century capitalist who regarded any restraint "as a despotic invasion of his constitutional rights" could not prevent considerations of public policy from altering the definition of the right to property. The police power has justified laws prohibiting men from engaging in certain occupations, from operating their factories under conditions described as unhealthy, from hiring whom they wished or from discriminating among the clients they served. Although the general scope of religious freedom has expanded, that has not prevented the denial of its protection to such groups as the Mormons who offended widely accepted principles of morality, although monogamy as an institution had no particular constitutional sanction.[32]

Finally, such widely cherished rights as those of habeas corpus or freedom of speech have in effect been suspended from time to time when other considerations seemed to make it desirable to do so.[33] The forced removal of Indians and Japanese Americans, as earlier of the Acadians, troubled the consciences of Americans particularly because the right of settlement and residence which may thus have been violated had no explicit constitutional guarantee.[34] It has also remained unclear to what extent a citizen surrenders his rights when he becomes a soldier or a seaman, voluntarily by enlistment or unwillingly through the draft.[35] The connotation of rights, even when enacted in constitutional form, has often passed through radical changes.

The rights of Americans did not constitute an impenetrable barrier against state action. They have been neither precisely defined nor immutable. What then has remained constant? Not the contents, but the conception of rights itself. Indeed, the very flexibility in adjusting to new conditions may well have strengthened the underlying idea that the citizen retained rights that set limits to the power of the state to act.

In this respect, the conception of rights did not depend upon formally elaborated procedures any more than did those of federalism or constitutionalism. On the contrary all three conceptions have been used as instruments to sustain and preserve the conviction that some limits on the power to govern were desirable.

The citizen who consented to be governed did not thereby totally deprive himself of the means of defense against the engine of coercion he thus created. He remained a human being, possessed of fears and aspirations, of hatreds and loves that had a dignity of their own that deserved respect even in the face of the organized procedures for the use of power in which he himself acquiesced.

The limits on state power were signs of that respect, and they therefore protected individuals, not groups, members, not associations. The legal fiction of corporate personality was necessary to extend that coverage to the body itself. But the arguments advanced by Calhoun that groups, as groups, had rights, received little support in the United States, because the abstract entities were not accorded the respect attached to the human personality, of which the restraints on the use of force were manifestations.[36]

In describing the development of liberty in the United States no formal array of rights is itself adequate as a criterion of freedom. Rather, it is necessary to examine first the extension or contraction of the limits on the capacity of government to act, then the procedures through which those limits were broadened or narrowed, and, above all, the purposes which those changes were designed to serve. For the proper use of power involved not only the assumption that it would operate through procedures embodying consent within recognized limits, but also the conviction that it would be used to achieve desirable ends.

☆ IV ☆
THE ENDS
OF
THE USE
OF
POWER

IN America the preservation of liberty called for the confinement of the instruments of coercion available to the state within recognized limits. But the boundaries between proper and improper use of political power were neither rigid nor immutable; they were subject to frequent adjustment under the pressure of changing conceptions of the ends of government action. To describe the development of freedom it is therefore necessary to examine the evolving purposes of the state that set the terms within which both its procedures and the limits on its operations took form.

The fundamental documents of the American polity generally began with a statement of the ends for the furtherance of which those present covenanted together: "for the glorie of God, and the advancement of the Christian faith, and honour of our king and countrie"; or "to form a more perfect union, establish justice, insure domestic tranquillity, provide for the common defense, promote the general welfare, and secure the blessings of liberty." The rhetoric of these professions must be interpreted in the light of underlying but un-expressed assumptions about the ends for which government was instituted among men. Some of these assumptions have remained constant for more than three hundred years; others have subtly but decisively been altered.[1]

The charter that brought the first American colony into being created a body politic and corporate, an entity en-dowed with the power to govern and with an identity apart from that of its members. Other factors prevented political theory in the New World, then or later, from taking on a Hegelian orientation. But for a century and a half after 1607 the political order matured without essential change in the conception of the state as a corporate body distinct from the individuals of which it was composed. The origin of many provinces in joint-stock companies and the practice of town settlement in New England accustomed Americans to the idea; and Harrington and other seventeenth-century writers gave them a theoretical framework within which to describe the operations of such a polity. By the time the Revolutionary generation sought a designation for the states it was estab-lishing, it was almost a matter of course that it should hit upon the term, Commonwealth, or, in its Latin, Republic.[2]

A state, John Locke pointed out, was not merely the aggregate of its constituent members but one body, like the family; and it therefore had interests of its own.[3] Some colonists gave the common ends preeminence over those of individuals. The Bible Commonwealths, for instance, were charged with a providential mission that overshadowed any personal objectives. But altogether apart from such mes-sianic considerations, it was of the essence of a Common-wealth that, having an identity of its own, it should also have ends of its own.[4]

Among such ends, it was repeatedly affirmed, were those of providing justice and securing the persons and the property of the inhabitants. By doing so the government served "the common good" which was, after all, the purpose for which the social contract had brought the state into being.[5]

The state did justice by using its power to adjudicate disputes among individuals. Impartially and on the basis of known principles, it decided who was right and who wrong in cases involving trespass, contract, property, and injury to persons. It awarded damages and had the means of compulsion to make its awards effective. By resolving the conflicts of one man with another, it contributed to the security of all. In these matters the government acted to reconcile the clash between the rights of one person and those of another. There was never any dispute as to the validity of its doing so.

The state took cognizance of another category of offenses which, although directed at individuals, disturbed the peace and thereby injured the whole community. By law it forbade a variety of felonies, and it took the initiative in ferreting out those who committed by word or deed that which the law forbade. It tried them for their crimes and meted out to the guilty appropriate chastisement, thus protecting the community against injury.[6]

In the seventeenth century the distinction between a wrong to an individual and an offense against the community was not entirely clear either as a concept or in administration. English experience, an imperfect acquaintance with the law, and practical convenience tended to blur the line between crime and tort, between larceny and trespass. A man who burned down his neighbor's barn might be punished if convicted of arson or might be ordered to pay damages if defeated in a suit of trespass. The circumstance that the same officials served in both capacities compounded the confusion; the term magistrate was comprehensive enough to include every type of administrator of government power. Furthermore some such functions might even be delegated to nongovernmental agencies.[7]

The distinction between criminal and civil law, between public and private offenses, between crimes and torts, emerged slowly and not always consistently. The accidental maiming of a person was a tort; if he died, it became manslaughter. In either case there was no question of the desirability for intervention by the state so long as it acted through procedures proper for the conviction of the guilty or the assessment of damages. That its actions resulted in the restriction of the liberty of criminals or trespassers was a necessary condition of sustaining the freedom of those against whom they directed their offenses.[8]

Another category of offenses, those which injured the whole community, involved the government more directly. The state was always accorded the right and duty of preserving itself. Even though it rested upon the consent of the governed it did not depend passively upon their acquiescence; it could use force to prevent its own destruction from within or without. It beat off external enemies by military power and internal ones through laws against treason and sedition.[9]

The struggle for survival in the early settlements frequently justified extreme measures. Nor did Americans begrudge their government the capacity to act in later emergencies; the suspension of the writ of habeas corpus during the Civil War, the encroachment upon the freedom of speech and the press in 1917, and the evacuation of the Japanese Americans in 1942, all expanded coercive power outside normal limits and procedures.[10]

The criteria for judging when danger was imminent were frequently unclear. Self-preservation could not be assured by simple defense against open attacks. The state was conceded the duty to be strong in advance of direct conflict, a duty defined in ever more comprehensive terms with the advance of technology and the changing character of war. But, if it could use power simply to strengthen itself in anticipation of emergency, could it not do so at any time? And, if so, what restraints prevented it from stamping out real or fancied opposition at will, as the Federalists were accused of doing by means of the Sedition Act of 1798?

Americans generally insisted upon the utility of some restraints even in emergencies and upon a contraction of powers after the crisis. But there have been times when many of them have been persuaded that the government could properly demand absolute conformity. Such changing needs and pressures repeatedly expanded and contracted the limits to which the state could go in defending itself.

Furthermore, military preparedness and the extirpation of opposition were themselves never considered adequate to preserve the government. In the seventeenth century, when the success or failure of every campaign was a direct manifestation of the benevolence or wrath of a Divine Providence, there was an evident connection between self-preservation and the God-fearing life of pious men. Afterward the ability to survive and prosper seemed dependent upon a growing population and a sound economy. Earlier or later the strength of the state rested upon the strength of the community so that the government had a stake in furthering the well-being of the whole social order.[11]

It was in reference to this last obligation that the views of the role of the state changed most radically in the course of American history. The assumptions that the government was to mediate in conflicts of individual rights, that it was to punish crimes against persons and property, and that it was to defend itself against direct assault remained constant. But the conception that political power was to further the welfare of the community, in the broader sense, by prohibiting harmful activities that might damage it spiritually, socially, and economically, passed through striking transformations in response to the altered conditions of life in the United States. As Jamestown became the tidewater South, as

Plymouth became industrial New England, the very conception of community changed, and, with it, the understanding of the ends that the government ought properly to pursue.

In the seventeenth century the salvation of a man's soul was as important an end of state action as the security of his body or his property. The preservation of godliness in the community was as urgent as the maintenance of military strength. The conduct of worship and the administration of the sacraments was in the custody of the church; but the government sustained the religious authorities by taxation and by punishing blasphemy, absence from services, heresy, and violations of the Sabbath. "These three things," wrote John Cotton in 1636, "do mutually and strongly maintain one another . . . authority in magistrates, liberty in people, purity in church."[12]

To the same end the state policed the family within which its members organized their personal lives. It expected that the household would ordinarily regulate itself but it stood ready to supply coercive sanctions for any delinquencies. It punished sexual offenses and violations of discipline; and it assumed oversight of the orphans, the indigent, and other individuals who lacked settled places. The government acted through a variety of officials and intermediary agencies, — tithingmen, selectmen, workhouses, and colleges — to secure social order.[13]

Finally, the state also concerned itself with the material well-being of the community. It forbade practices considered deleterious such as frauds in commercial transactions, forestalling, and monopoly; it established markets and the conditions for their operations; and it set prices for some commodities and regulated the conditions of labor. The justification for all such measures was the necessity for restraining individuals from behavior dangerous to the community.[14]

The state, in pursuing the common good, was not limited to the essentially negative task of making and enforcing prohibitory laws. It could also take positive steps toward the same goal. Americans of the seventeenth and eighteenth centuries used the term Commonwealth literally. The wealth of a Republic was common in the sense that it belonged to the whole rather than to any of its particular components. Such a state therefore had an economic interest of its own to defend and develop, apart from the sum of the particular interests of the individuals within it.

Until the Revolution, the relation with England and the sovereignty of the Crown had obscured the conception. While some provinces already acted in accordance with it, not even Rhode Island or Connecticut, the least subject to external restraint, could openly give it expression. Independence dissolved all such inhibitions. The free Republics of the United States were then in a position to advance their common interests. Now having a polity of their own, they could use power to do so.[15]

It was true that the state faced difficult questions of policy when it came to defining the common interest and the means by which to further it. It had to make choices among competing goals in order to serve as a directing force in the economy. In consequence, it favored some types of enterprise over others by intervening directly in their operations. When it judged that banks or canals furthered the common interest, it participated in their development, which was as much an end of government as the maintenance of a military force or of a postal system or of a network of roads.[16]

In the course of its intervention the state aided some individuals, groups, and sections, and injured others, so that the process of arriving at actual decisions often entailed the conflict of diverse interests. More important, its participation often took the form of the grant of precisely those privileges that in other contexts seemed to be but survivals of feudalism.

Monopolies, bounties, patents, and charters of incorporation now were justified by the fact that they served the common interests of the community rather than the particular interests of individuals.

The ends of government in a Commonwealth were as wide as the community itself. The organized use of power, whether to prevent offenses or to encourage desirable spiritual and material development, intruded in every aspect of life. The state therefore was not content merely to judge among men in dispute; it also acted positively to further its own ends as the community defined them. The greater common good which served the liberty of all justified whatever restrictions on the rights of individuals its action entailed.

Long before the Revolution other forces were taking form that would ultimately clash with the Commonwealth conception. No matter what the theory, American life in fact discouraged the survival of coherent communities in which there was general agreement on the ends and means of social action. By the end of the seventeenth century, the process of settlement had introduced a variety of cultures and religions into the mainland colonies and even in New England had dissolved the uniformity of the first decades. Thereafter the growing diversity of the population began to raise practical challenges to the idea that there were common goals toward which the government could strive. The breakdown of the older assumptions was slowest where the distinct groups lived apart as did the Moravians of North Carolina, or the Catholics of Maryland; it accelerated when they lived together as did Quakers, Baptists, Jews, and Lutherans in Newport or Philadelphia.[17]

The consequences of the breakdown emerged slowly and were imperfectly understood by contemporaries. The earliest reaction was not to discard the idea that the state had ends of its own, but to narrow the scope of those ends to such matters upon which common agreement actually existed. By the middle of the eighteenth century there was *de facto* toleration of all religious sects in the colonies; by the end of the century there was effective equality among them. But, although a few thinkers from Roger Williams to James Madison had already argued for complete separation of church and state, the government continued to intervene in the religious life of its citizens on into the nineteenth century.[18]

Practical exigencies and revolutionary ideology combined to strengthen the same trend in many spheres of life. No group was strong enough throughout the new nation to impose its will upon all the others; and the conceptions of freedom of choice so heatedly debated in the 1770's inhibited the impulse to use force to restrain the individual. Men who had just fought British invasions of their own rights had to give a respectful hearing to any plea that used the same terms of justification. Responsiveness to such pleas led the government to avoid inequality in the treatment of its citizens rather than to abstain from any action at all.

In the fifty years after independence, the state continued to act as if it had an obligation to develop the productive system by favorable legislation, and by grants of bounties, monopolies, and acts of incorporation. The critical modification in its role came in the acknowledgment that it ought not to be selective in the bestowal of those privileges, but ought to make them equally available to all seekers. The state still had the right and duty to charter banks or aid in the construction of canals, but it was not to discriminate among conflicting interests any more than among conflicting religious sects; it was to aid them all.[19]

The gradual adoption of this acquiescent policy changed the relation of government to enterprise. Privileges lost a good deal of their value when they became generally accessible. The corporation chartered under a general law was no longer the distinctive body it had been when created by special act; and a monopoly took on a new meaning when shared by several competitors.

The proliferation of such grants eased the adjustment when, in time, a general assault was launched upon the whole system of privilege. The complex crusade which reached its climax in the 1830's was ostensibly directed against monopoly, although in any realistic sense that was no longer a feature of the American economy. Those who used the anti-monopoly slogan found it a convenient way of describing their actual intention, that of supplanting the existing pattern of government involvement in the economy in favor of other forms more in accord with their interests. That broader design accounted for the fact that in the United States, although nowhere else, the battle over monopoly acquired distinct ethical overtones.

The miscellaneous groups which enlisted in the campaign objected to the restraints state action still imposed upon economic growth. The United States in 1830 had no equivalent of the Bank of England; anyone with capital could start a note-issuing bank. But the power of the Bank of the United States as fiscal agent and government depository to expand and contract currency enabled it to exert a marked influence upon the nation's credit. That, rather than its nonexistent monopoly, antagonized those of Jackson's partisans who sought a total dissolution of the connection between the state and the banking system. Antipathy to practices which seemed feudal in origin, the heritage of eighteenth-century fears of any massive consolidation of power, and the swift social changes that accompanied territorial and economic expansion accentuated the hostility to privilege on the part of those whose interests the system damaged.[20]

Although the supporters of the American System for a time clung to the Commonwealth conception in an attenuated form, the opponents of privilege ultimately secured the rejection of the whole idea. In the course of their long conflict, the foes of monopoly denied that the state could be regarded as distinct from the people who composed it; it had no interest of its own, but existed simply to serve its citizens. Its actions could no longer be justified by reference to a common interest; they had to be weighed in terms of their effect upon the welfare of the aggregate of citizens. A democratic Republic could not dispose of favors, even if those were universally accessible. It could act to the advantage of society only by assuring individuals of security in person and property to enable them to seek their own ends as effectively as possible.[21]

The collapse of the Commonwealth conception in the middle of the nineteenth century led to a reinterpretation of the role of the state. The only measures which truly contributed to the general welfare were those in which the government abjured a positive role and confined itself to establishing regulations to protect its citizens.

The altered definition presented problems of its own, for it was not possible to transfer the notion of police which had prevailed in the homogeneous community of the past to the rapidly changing economic and social conditions of the second half of the nineteenth century. Urbanization and industrialization hastened the transformation of the old communities so that it was increasingly difficult to conceive of coherent ends which police power could serve. The great new cities and factories functioned through impersonal relationships; the roles of citizen, taxpayer, laborer, employer were defined without reference to the individual characteristics of the men who filled them, and the government could not deal with them in any but an impersonal way.

The business of police, no matter how defined, involved compulsion which in the seventeenth and eighteenth centuries had been administered by elected officials guided by commonly agreed upon standards. Compulsion took on quite another aspect in the complex, changing communities of the nineteenth century, composed as they were of heterogeneous populations, reft by internal differences, and obliged to enforce the law with a professional bureaucracy not representative of the people and often controlled by only a single group. The city of 1850 needed more effective means of apprehending murderers and thieves than the village of 1750; yet the enforcement of Sabbath-observance laws by professional police officers seemed tyrannical at the later date as it did not at the earlier. The principles by which the assize of bread was established in the eighteenth century did not serve for setting railroad rates in the nineteenth. Under such conditions there were no widely accepted criteria of how much regulation was necessary or useful for security, or of whether the appropriate standards were to be to the advantage of the whole society or of some measurable fraction of it.

Hence the growing demand that the state apply its power only in a restricted province of law within which there was general agreement, as in the suppression of crimes of violence. Outside that area was the province of individual freedom where the rule of personal conscience was to be unrestrained. In these matters which concerned only the individual, the state was to abstain from any effort to set general goals. There was no reason, Mill wrote in a widely read formulation, why "all human existence should be constructed on some one or some small number of patterns." Each person was the best judge of his own mode of laying out his existence.[22] In all but a very narrow range of activities the government was to refrain even from most police regulations through which it had formerly interfered in the lives of the citizens. Individual initiative, discipline, and philanthropy were to rule in practically all social experience.

In some cases, the line of separation between the areas in which the state was to act and those in which it abstained emerged quite consistently. Although anachronistic provisions against blasphemy and in favor of Sunday observance persisted, the separation of church and state proceeded steadily after 1776, supported by the provisions of the federal and state constitutions and the Fourteenth Amendment.[23]

There was a similar trend toward the divorce of the state from the economy. In addition to the elimination of the directing, goal-setting role of the government, there was steady pressure to convert its regulatory police functions from positive to passive forms. Darwinian assumptions about the survival of the fittest were modified by the belief that the course of evolution led away from coercive military activities and toward productive, peaceful ones. Faith in progress toward an enterprising future led to continuing demands for the contraction of governmental power. The self-adjusting capacity of the free competitive market would take its place in regulating the affairs of modern men. This was the context within which the idea gradually evolved that insecurity, except from violence, was itself a condition of freedom and of progress and was worth preserving as a stimulant. That was a further reason why the government should make as few moves as possible.[24]

The logic of this argument implied that there were no crimes in the economic sphere, only torts. The state was to take no action on its own behalf; it was an impartial arbiter among the various contending groups in the society, operating only to resolve disputes and to regulate the fair behavior of individuals, with no intrinsic interest of its own. It enforced contracts when asked to do so by injured parties, and made available information by which individuals might guide themselves. If it set rates or prosecuted conspiracies, it was not on the basis of its own concern with just price or stable market, but as a result of appeals to it by shippers or competitors damaged by unfair practices. The Interstate Commerce Act embodied these assumptions; and the early regulatory commissions were inclined to interpret their quasi-judicial roles in these terms. Patents ceased to be privileges granted by the state for its own ends and became rights which it merely registered. The development of laissez-faire thought thus equated liberty with the denial of the propriety of any autonomous government action. When William Graham Sumner insisted, in the 1880's, that society did "not need any care or supervision," that laissez faire was "nothing but the doctrine of liberty," he had moved a long way not only from the Hamiltonian conception of the state's positive, directing role but also from that of an active policing function.[25]

Not all established governmental practices could be brought into accord with this altered conception of the ends of state action. Contrary tendencies, inherited from the past, often gained strength from other social developments and impeded the application of laissez-faire doctrine. The vague humanitarianism of the eighteenth century, of which the Quakers had been exemplars, now was charged with fresh emotional and intellectual power as the belief in the perfectibility of man offered an increasingly attractive secular equivalent for old faiths. Those who held a firm conviction in the capacity of man to rise to ever higher forms had at first expected that he would do so through the voluntary exercise of benevolence. But, by the middle of the nineteenth century, the reformers had come to expect the state to use its police power in order to remove the obstacles to human improvement. This impulse also received support of a sort from the Benthamite principle that the criterion of government action was the greatest good for the greatest number.[26]

Furthermore, it appeared that the removal of governmental restraints was not itself always enough to permit the unimpeded operation of free individual forces. Early in the nineteenth century, the opponents of monopoly, which was then grounded in grants from the government, had sought relief by ending interference by the state. In the last quarter of the century, however, when monopoly seemed to spring from a voluntary process of industrial concentration, they found it necessary to turn to the government to police the operations of the "predatory capitalists."[27]

The result was a contradictory effort to extend rather than to contract the police power. In some matters, as in the spread of philanthropy into a variety of new spheres, this entailed little interference with personal rights. To the degree that the voluntary agencies which had assumed the responsibility for the care of indigent and dependent persons proved inadequate, the state continued and expanded its traditional concern with the helpless members of society.[28]

In other matters, greater government activity intruded into those spheres which theorists had designated as reserved to personal discretion. The line that writers like Mill drew in the abstract could not be maintained in practice. Pressure from a variety of sources led the states first to expand their police regulations and then to formulate general goals that justified them in positive action.[29]

Education was thus a requisite of citizenship. As a result it seemed plausible that the government should require some schooling for every child. That did not at first mean that the state was to operate educational institutions although it compelled students to attend, whatever their own wishes or those of their parents. But in time the requirement by the government became an obligation upon it to support or to operate the schools.[30]

Analogous trends appeared in many other matters. Disease was a menace to the community; therefore the state was to outlaw noxious conditions, to provide water and sewerage systems, to regulate the sale of milk and other goods, to inspect or build proper housing, to zone structures with the intention of preserving access to light and air, whatever property or personal rights might be interfered with thereby. For similar reasons the government was also to legislate morality by prohibiting gambling, unacceptable sexual behavior, the sale of alcoholic beverages, and the distribution of pornography. Certain enterprises performed public services; therefore they were to operate under franchises and their rates were to be regulated.[31]

The effort to define these measures as legitimate objectives of government met fierce resistance not only from individuals whose interests were adversely affected but also from those concerned with preserving the areas of personal and propertied freedom. The conflict inevitably arrayed differing conceptions of freedom against each other. The arguments of justification and attack cannot be understood in terms of the extent to which these measures actually infringed upon individual rights abstractly defined. Rather, they were the outgrowth of a confused situation in which the community could no longer formulate a single goal toward which a commonwealth could strive.[32]

In the last two decades of the nineteenth century a reaction to that situation produced demands that the government act to restore unity, direction, and order to the economy and to the whole society. The evils of unrestrained expansion and its concomitant problems in the nation's farms and cities led some Americans to suppose that concerted communal action would be more likely to supply remedies than the efforts of unguided individuals. Such sentiments fed a growing body of support for the alternative of socialism.

That attitude had been anticipated earlier in the century by the handfuls of visionaries who established utopian communities in which common ownership of property and control of production attempted to restore to society the wholeness of the family. These experiments had been brief in duration, except where they had drawn on religious sanctions for support. But their failure did not discourage later theorists who wished to expand the ends of the state to include the ownership and operation of the means of production.[33]

In the 1880's the current of socialist ideas was fed from both domestic and foreign sources. Edward Bellamy was the most popular American writer who expounded the virtues of a nationally owned economy; and the European socialists had a perceptible influence. Then, and for some time later, socialism seemed to be but the extreme of American radicalism. The Socialist Party, expressly dedicated to that program, grew steadily to reach the height of its voting strength in 1912. In addition, significant elements in the populist and progressive movements espoused some aspects of the socialist program, particularly the government ownership of transportation and communications, and the program which became known as municipal socialism. From this point of view the surrender of property rights was a means for securing the other rights of the individual. The full-blown socialist argued that common ownership would liberate man from social oppression; those who did not go the whole way, urged that limited government control of utilities would free all other forms of enterprise.[34]

These ideas were only temporarily attractive. After 1912, the influence of socialism waned. The collapse of the Socialist Party may have been due, in part at least, to its hostility to war in 1917 which led to its condemnation as unAmerican. More significant was the general decline of the sentiment in favor of even limited kinds of state ownership, revealed in the aftermath of the war with the restoration of the railroads to private possession. The history of the American telephone and telegraph systems, in this respect, offers an interesting contrast both to the post office of the United States and to European practice. Thereafter, although such problems as those of urban rapid transit produced new demands for government ownership, it was not for ideological but for pragmatic reasons.[35]

Socialism failed as a doctrine in the United States because of a persistent conviction among Americans that private property ought to remain secure from the government. The state was always accorded the power to take property through the constitutionally defined methods of eminent domain; and taxation was sometimes conceived as a means of regulating and policing the use of property to implement a particular theory as in the cases of the single tax and the income tax. But neither Henry George nor the proponents of the income tax intended to make a general assault on private property; and the adoption of the measures they favored was not a sign of the strength of socialism and may even have weakened its appeal.[36]

Apart from these exceptions there was a general reluctance to permit the state to interfere with the right of individual possession. A nation in which property was widely diffused among freeholding farmers, small businessmen, and artisans, one in which success as an ideal and social mobility as a reality kept alive the prospect of ownership for large sectors of the population, did not offer fertile soil for the spread of socialist ideas.

In any case, by 1920, discontented Americans found greater attractiveness in roads to reform that left private property untouched. The early decades of the century had witnessed the emergence of a rival conception of the role of government. Although the state itself was not to own or control the means of production, it was to assume a general supervision of the economy by taking the responsibility for planning.

These ideas found expression in the writings of such men as Lester Ward, John Dewey, and Herbert Croly. Unwilling to accept the proposition that the human will was helpless in the face of impersonal evolutionary forces, these thinkers insisted that it was possible to apply intelligence to social problems through planning, which would give precedence to communal over personal interests. "The individual has reigned long enough," Ward announced. He would have to relinquish some of his rights for the larger good as society took its affairs into its own hands and shaped its own destinies.[37]

The burgeoning conservation movement ascribed the disastrous depletion of the nation's resources to the lack of planning. "The period in which individualism was patriotism in this country has passed by," wrote Charles Van Hise. "The time has come when individualism must become subordinate to responsibility to the many." From that position it was not far to the denial of the right to marry and to bear children wihout the consent of the eugenicist who planned the future of the population. "As a first very moderate step toward the development of the stamina of the human race, defectives should be precluded from continuing the race," Van Hise asserted.[38]

In the first two decades of the twentieth century, planning was still a vague idea espoused by people who held many different views of the ends of state action — socialists, humanitarians, politicians like Theodore Roosevelt, proponents of scientific legislation like Brooks Adams, and bankers like George Perkins, who were eager for economic order. They had in common only the vigorous opposition of the defenders of laissez faire. That opposition and the lack of appropriate mechanisms for putting such schemes into effect confined the discussion largely to the ideological plane.[39]

During the First World War government planning moved from the realm of theory to that of practice. The War Industries Board not only set important precedents for the future but also had a direct influence upon some aspects of the structure of American industry. In the 1920's these activities shrank in importance, but businessmen continued to collaborate with friendly administrations in setting federal reserve policy and in furthering overseas trade and shipping.[40]

During the eight years of the New Deal the scope of planning expanded rapidly, although without over-all foresight or conscious direction. The NRA, the fiscal policy embarked upon through deficit spending, the TVA and the AAA, rural resettlement, and a multitude of other activities all showed the same inclination toward giving the government power to plan for the productive system.[41]

The effects of the Second World War were even greater than those of the First, both because precedents already existed and because the crisis was more extreme. Monetary, credit, and production controls, price fixing, and rationing, were all evidence of growing state power. Despite some opposition, features of these emergency measures lingered on into the postwar period. In addition, the federal government assumed responsibility in the Act of 1946 for using "all its plans, functions, and resources" to "promote maximum employment, production, and purchasing power." Later it also took on some obligations with regard to adequate housing and orderly urban expansion. Although the intent of the laws was not implemented as fully as their sponsors wished, this line of legislation revealed a broad expansion of the conception of the role of the government in the economy.[42]

Despite the insistence of some American thinkers that, given the narrow limits of collective rationality, the government ought to confine itself to creation of a framework for free enterprise, the welfare state acquired unprecedented new obligations in other spheres also. The range of what it owed its citizens in social security, medical care, education, and housing expanded enormously; and such services were no longer confined to the indigent or dependent, but extended to become a normal part of the life of every American.[43]

The question frequently raised was whether every citizen did not thereby become dependent upon the government, with a consequent loss in his own freedom. "Freedom from want and fear," argued a philosopher, "is more than a demand for liberty, for it demands insurance and protection by provident institutions, which imply the dominance of a paternal government, with artificial privileges secured by law. This would be freedom from the dangers of a free life. It shows us liberty contracting its field and bargaining for safety first."[44]

The broadened conception of the ends of the state had undoubtedly contracted the rights and narrowed the range of choices of some individuals. But the questions that remain to be answered are whether those losses have been offset by gains in personal liberty through freedom from cares, and what the consequences will be of the new balance between social and individual power.

The long development from the commonwealth conception to the idea of the state as arbiter, and from that to the welfare state, has had unique American characteristics. In Europe, too, seventeenth-century governments had assumed the power to direct the whole life of society. But the state there was the Crown and the privileges of which it disposed went to limited groups of aristocrats and great merchants. By contrast, the state in the New World quickly became the whole body of the people by whose consent government operated. Privileges could not be confined to a small sector of the population; and their widespread diffusion deprived them of their restrictive character.

The liberal demand for a divorce between the state on the one hand, and the economic and social activities of society on the other, took a distinctive form in the United States. It was not necessary to attack the entrenched holders of privilege as it was in Europe but merely to slough off practices that had already largely lost their meaning. That, rather than the absence of an ideology of feudalism, was responsible for the easy transformations in the nineteenth-century conceptions of the ends of the state in America.[45]

In Europe, the attack upon privilege was revolutionary and demanded an alliance with significant groups opposed to the system of private property. That established a basis for the twentieth-century growth of socialism. By contrast, the attack upon privilege in the United States opened out into a system of free private enterprise which has survived despite the modifications of the past half-century. There has been no equivalent in the United States to the forms of state ownership and control characteristic of even the most conservative European countries.

An analogous pattern of development has shaped the relations of government to the other spheres of social action. The seventeenth-century modes of using power to control religious, family, cultural, and intellectual life dissolved in the United States with relatively little strain, and that permitted the almost effortless evolution of new forms, responsive to the needs of the people of the Republic.

Changes in the conceptions of the ends of power have proceeded within a context of parallel transformations in the procedures of, and limitations upon, its use. Whenever, as at the present time, men have had to grapple with the problems posed by the state's assumption of new obligations or its relinquishment of old ones, they have had to operate within the framework of their own understanding of the proper modes of coercive action. The resultant tension was a condition of American liberty.

Changes in the ends of the use of power through government in themselves neither contracted nor extended liberty.

Whether their influence was exerted in one direction or another depended also upon the procedures employed and the limits of action recognized.

The obligation to folow proper procedures, the acceptance of limits, and the conviction that power was to serve desirable ends have formed a triangular configuration of forces within which the increase or decrease of liberty may be assessed. The ultimate criterion is the capacity of men to act, whether through the coercive instruments of government or otherwise. The procedures, the limits, and the ends of their use of power are measures of the extent to which the state expands their capabilities while still leaving them able to act, if they wish, through other means.

☆ V ☆
VOLUNTARY
ASSOCIATIONS

To BE free, men sought to organize power so that it would be used only in accordance with their wills. They aimed to achieve a balance of restraints by vesting the means of compulsion in the state, to be exercised within defined procedures and limits and directed toward accepted goals. The assumption that the polity could operate only in agreed-upon ways and toward agreed-upon ends protected individuals against the consequences of the unrestrained use of force and extended their liberty. As a result, the policeman's stick generally remained in abeyance and the government could usually act through persuasion or education.

The coercive methods of the state — actual or potential — were not the only ones through which men sought to achieve their common objectives. As individuals or in groups they retained the capacity for acting through other forms, so long as they did so without the sanctions of violence reserved to the government. Such nonpolitical modes of action necessarily depended upon the ability to elicit spontaneous cooperation or acquiescence. The emergence of a distinctive pattern of voluntary association was inextricably bound in with the history of liberty in America for it created a significant range of alternatives to the use of coercive power through the state.

The voluntary association appeared early in American history. From the eighteenth century onward it developed steadily in importance and its subtle influence upon both the political and nonpolitical activities of society profoundly affected the scope of freedom in the United States. The churches, the universities, and the banks which adopted the patterns of voluntary association in the New World had European antecedents. But they acquired their distinctive character by disentangling themselves from the political ties in which their counterparts had become enmeshed in the Old World.

By the seventeenth century the growth of the centralized state in England and on the continent had subjected every type of association to the overreaching authority of the sovereign. Political theory had long since established "the notion that the State" was "an exclusive Community," the "all-comprehensive, and therefore the one and only, expression of that common life which" stood "above the life of the individual." Within that view there was no room "for States within the State," and "all the smaller groups had to be brought under the rubric 'Communes and Corporations.'" Ecclesiastical and educational bodies, guilds and mercantile companies, sought or accepted links to the government in order to use its sanctions to protect or extend their privileges; and the Crown, in turn, found these agencies useful means of strengthening its own hegemony.[1]

A multitude of associations became bodies politic or arms of the government, either by charter or by the supposition that immemorial custom had made them so. Religious, educational, cultural, philanthropic, and business institutions alike were assumed to act under the authority of the sovereign and endowed with privileges in return for their assimilation to the state apparatus. Only the disadvantaged or the insignificant remained apart — the schools and chapels of the dissenting sects, small family business firms, and the like.[2]

Roger Williams had vainly protested against these connections. He argued that churches, like the colleges of physicians or the companies of East India and Turkey merchants or any other societies, might operate as they wished without in the least impairing or disturbing the peace of the community, the essence or being of which was entirely distinct from these particular societies. He envisioned a complex of autonomous bodies operating without restraint or privilege toward their own particular goals in their own ways.[3]

The dominant trends in the seventeenth-century state were, however, altogether hostile to such pleas. The ties between the Crown and various types of associations grew stronger rather than weaker. As a result, many privileged bodies became instruments of the Old Regime and suffered from the general attack upon privilege in the eighteenth and nineteenth centuries. The critics, reformers, and revolutionaries, who assailed the establishment in all its aspects, generally sought to dissolve these bodies which, in their view, were but branches of an anachronistic system of government. The degree to which the assault succeeded varied from country to country, but everywhere the institutional structure was transformed.

In the new regimes, the functions once served by the church or the university or the chartered company were either to be supplied by the individual alone or directly by the state. These were the two alternatives; there seemed no acceptable intermediate principle of action. When corporative theory later called attention to other levels of organization, it regarded them as embraced within the organic state.[4]

In the United States quite another process established the voluntary association as an important mode of social behavior. There conditions conspired to develop the voluntary association as Roger Williams had envisioned it. The attack on privilege had other results in the New World because the links of these bodies to the state had already by then acquired a character different from that in Europe.

By the eighteenth century such groups in the colonies had already established the capacity to act with or without the explicit grant of a charter. The assemblies sometimes arrogated the power to incorporate municipalities, boards of trustees for schools, hospitals, workhouses, loan offices, churches, and water supply, insurance, and trading companies. They did so in response to a felt need and without regard for legal niceties. That procedure often evoked objections from the royal authorities and therefore could not be used with impunity.

More generally, voluntary associations took form without legal sanction. Religious bodies came to act like corporations whether they were entitled to do so or not. The Crown frowned upon the formal grant of charters to any but the established church; yet a variety of devices permitted other sects to act as if they were incorporated. By the same token, the invalidation of its charter proved no burden to Harvard College, and undertakers of iron and glass works, of fishing and trading ventures, found the means of carrying on their activities without acts of incorporation. That the Crown frowned upon such activities also was manifested by the extension of the Bubble Act to the colonies in 1741. Yet it was impossible to control the formation of these spontaneous bodies which had the approval or tolerance of local authorities.[5]

By 1770 a multitude of such entities were functioning. The difference between the incorporated ones and unincorporated ones was legally real; and the privilege of a charter was coveted. But, since the attainment of that privilege was laden with difficulty, men learned to do without it. What was characteristic of towns was characteristic of other associations as well. "The line between the true corporations" and those improperly so designated was "exceedingly difficult to draw." The terms "incorporate," "corporation," "body politic," and "charter" were all used "with the greatest looseness."[6]

The pre-Revolutionary pattern of development had emerged most clearly with regard to the religious establishment. Nineteenth-century observers were impressed with the ability of Americans to evade those problems of church and state which had been responsible for "half the wars in Europe, half the internal troubles" that vexed the Old World. "This whole vast chapter of debate and strife" remained unopened in the United States, commented Lord Bryce. All religious bodies, when he wrote in 1885, were "absolutely equal before the law, and unrecognized by the law, except as voluntary associations of private citizens."[7]

This fortunate condition was the product of a long historical development. The first churches in the New World were as closely tied to the state as those in the Old; the separation was not formally to be achieved until after Independence. Yet by 1776 American religious bodies had already in many respects become voluntary associations.[8]

The diversity of the American population and the erosion of the old tight communities contributed to that outcome. In cities like Philadelphia, New York, and Newport a variety of sects coexisted harmoniously; and in few colonies was there a precise identification of religious affiliation with social status. It was not possible therefore to justify preferential treatment for one as against the others. The widespread hostility that prevented the creation of an Anglican episcopate reflected that sentiment; and contradictory carry-overs from earlier or from English practice were regarded as anachronisms that would wither away as a matter of course.

The changing conception of the church prevented an accommodation to permit equality of treatment for all sects within the framework of the establishment, as England and

Canada later did. The congregational bias present in Puritanism from the start and the conception of the church as a free body of believers, popularized by the Quakers and the Baptists, soon led to a rejection of any form of coercive state intervention.

Finally, practical conditions encouraged voluntarism. In the New World the distinction between the established, government-related associations and the purely voluntary ones was far less consequential than in the Old World. Through trusteeship or other devices, all the churches acquired the capacity for holding property. The multiple jurisdictions of the various colonies prevented any single institution from achieving a totally dominant situation. There were few significant disabilities or advantages to affiliation with one group as against another. Everything was new, improvised, and poor. Church, chapel, and synagogue were much alike in their appearance and situation. Privilege was of but paltry value; subsidies and endowments were less consequential than the loyalty and contributions of persuaded members, as the Anglicans discovered in their contest with other sects in the eighteenth century. Under these conditions, the practical advantages of voluntary actions went far toward compensating for any gains from establishment.

To a considerable degree the same conditions obtained in other spheres of social action. Education, philanthropy, and business all felt a pragmatic pressure toward voluntary organization. Promoters who set on foot ventures to trade with the Indians, to speculate in land, to operate bridges, roads, ferries, and libraries, or to promote commerce and culture continued to believe that ties to the state and the ability to use government sanctions were valuable; and some enterprises sought incorporation. But such links to the polity were by no means essential; and the failure to secure them did not alone consign a project to oblivion. In most cases the projects could be carried through in other ways.

A serious issue arose only when such action clashed clearly with imperial policy, as it did in the struggle for control of the currency. The sponsors of the Massachusetts banks, rebuffed by the Governor in their quest for charters, proceeded to issue notes on their own, and were only restrained from continuing to do so by positive parliamentary action. The subordinate position and incomplete sovereignty of the colonies prevented a decisive test of the extent to which voluntary action would have been effective in banking as in other spheres.[9]

This was the situation on the eve of the Revolution which made such a test possible. Independence created powerful new governments which confronted an immediate dilemma. On the one hand, they assumed that they were to set about creating corporations like those of the Old World — agencies of the state endowed with political attributes to serve some public function. On the other hand, practical conditions prevented them from making choices or granting effective monopolies.

These privileges, in the United States, could not be justified by reference to the interests or preferences of a monarch. In a Republic they were tolerable only insofar as they served the interests of the whole people; and independence set off a quest for a workable way of furthering the welfare of the Commonwealth through the use of privilege.

In practice, American society had by then lost the capacity for agreeing upon a definition of the common interest in many critical matters. In actuality, community life was fragmented among a variety of groups divided by ethnic, religious, sectional, and economic lines; and none had preeminence enough to identify its own, with the common, interest. It had long since become impossible to associate with the community one church or one enterprise, as one could one state. The inability to do so had already made nonsectarianism the only means of concerted action in some matters. The community could not support a specific church, but it could support religion in general.[10]

The broad consequences of the inability to define a common interest emerged in the quarter-century after 1776. The eager entrepreneurs who turned to the states for the privilege of incorporation quickly found that its expected advantages eluded them. It was no more possible to confine the benefits of incorporation to a single bank or a single university than to a single church. The fear of a monopoly on the part of a bank or a university in the 1780's and 1790's was identical with that of a monopoly by a church.[11] The result was a significant adjustment. The state granted charters to associations which sought them, but proved incapable of discriminating among applicants. Each grant became a precedent for its successors. When Massachusetts established a new bank in Salem or a new college in the District of Maine, it could not deny the same privilege to Newburyport or to Berkshire County. The number of charters proliferated. As the Commonwealth ideal faded, any church or school or business enterprise could seek and attain the advantages of incorporation.

Such associations were neither privileged nor exclusive — were not established in the European sense. They were therefore spared the brunt of the attack by the underprivileged or aggrieved elements in society who fought not association as such, but monopoly. Furthermore these associations depended for their success not on externally endowed powers but on the ability to elicit and to manage effectively the support of their members. Between 1770 and 1820 the patterns outlined in the eighteenth century were clearly defined. Churches, schools, philanthropic, social and business organizations sought and secured incorporation freely as the government surrendered the power to select among applicants and as the charter ceased to bring with it any exclusive privileges. The corporation ceased to be an agency of the state and became even more clearly simply a more convenient way in which an association could conduct its own affairs.[12]

After 1820, the growing pluralism and expansiveness of American society encouraged every type of associational activity. Corporations had become private bodies which differed from less formally constituted societies only in the details of their organization. Whether promoters chose one mode of organization or another became a matter of their own convenience; and general incorporation laws eliminated the last element of governmental selectivity. Before very long any group could secure a charter, although not all sought to do so because other types of organizational arrangement were also attractive. Consequently, the great variety of forms available for cooperative action enabled men to satisfy numerous social needs by voluntary efforts.[13]

The immense proliferation of associations was in part a product of the mid-nineteenth-century fragmentation of the American community and, in part, a result of the increased ethnic diversity of the population produced by internal and foreign migration. Needs which could no longer be met by a whole community acting through the state were now satisfied by narrower voluntary associations. Although paradoxically, the few existing formal studies have dealt with the problems of the foreign-born, the behavior of natives — the Yankees for example — as they moved to the West and to the cities was remarkably similar.

All people in motion quickly became sensitive to their inability to deal with problems that extended beyond their own persons. They formed associations to provide the round of ritual and the patterns of reaffirmed belief of which the churches were custodians, to guard against the dependency of individuals in the face of death, disease, and poverty, and to preserve cultures that supplied them with emotional and aesthetic satisfaction. The need to belong to a group, whatever function it served, also influenced such men. They sought a sense of anchorage through identification with some larger entity, hoping to offset the effects of the unsettling elements in American life. In all groups, churches, mutual-aid societies, and fraternal orders helped to fix the role of the individual in the society in which he lived.[14]

The character of economic enterprise reflected the same splintering tendencies. After 1820, the business corporation was not considered different from other ways of doing business by virtue of any general communal end. Like other corporations, it served the interests of its members; in that respect it was simply a more convenient type of private company.

The growth in the number of associations and the transformation of the corporation into a purely voluntary agency heightened the importance of attempts to emphasize its private character and to relieve it of the danger of interference by the government. To mark its separation from the state it was necessary to obscure the public attributes which had originally been inherent in the character of the corporation. A tortuous succession of legal opinions, judicial decisions, and legislative acts attempted to establish the inviolability of the private corporation from government interference. The critical points were the Dartmouth College Case, the Charles River Bridge Case, and the ultimate judicial interpretations of the Fourteenth Amendment. This line of decisions established the corporation as a private entity, created by a contract which the state could not modify, and endowed with private rights upon which the state could not intrude. Significantly, these cases involved first religious and educational, and then business, bodies. These developments affirmed the legal personality of the incorporated body; but by setting it apart from state control, they strengthened its voluntary attributes and made it all but identical with the unincorporated association.[15]

Nineteenth-century Americans, however, were inclined to emphasize the private rather than the voluntary features of the corporation. No doubt they took its voluntary nature for granted. More important, obsessed as they were with the necessity for making the distinction between public and private spheres of action, they were tempted to identify the corporation as a private entity concerned with such affairs as business or religion from which the state was excluded.

Yet, since the unifying conception of the Commonwealth had by then disappeared it was not possible to draw the line between public and private precisely or clearly. Only in the most general terms could Americans argue that there was a sharp distinction between the public and private bodies when it came to spheres of activity, forms of control, and property rights. Abstractly speaking, the private corporation was concerned with specific limited objectives; and it was composed of stockholders who held shares of its property and who elected its directors. On the other hand, a public body operated toward general goals, was composed of members who did not have a direct property interest in it, and was managed by elected officials.

This distinction described the difference between the business corporation and the government. But it was by no means adequate to classify all activities as either private or public. The forces that made some forms of transportation or education public and others private were largely local and specific, never categorical. A consistent flexibility of arrangements in the nineteenth century emphasized the performance of a task rather than the form of organization. Schools and hospitals could be both public and private; the decisions were shaped by pragmatic considerations rather than by doctrinaire assumptions.

Nor did the distinction between the member who chose directors and the citizens who elected officials pivot entirely upon the possession of a property interest. The members of hospitals, universities, or private corporations could no more turn the property of the institutions of which they were custodians to their own use than could citizens appropriate the public possessions of the community. It was not about such attributes that the actual distinction between the private association and the public, governmental body turned, but upon the voluntary fragmented character of the former and the compulsory, inclusive character of the latter.[16]

The discussion of the private nature of the corporation was most sharply focused when it came to problems peculiar to business corporations. Ambiguity as to the status of hospitals or universities and the inability to locate them in a precisely articulated structure of institutions, for the moment created few difficulties. In a general sense, they served the public good, under whatever auspices they operated; and the need for their services justified the disorderly overlapping of functions.

By contrast, the desire to mark out the purely private character of the business corporation ultimately ensnared its defenders in troublesome complications. After 1820, this had become the critical instrument of American economic development. Its promoters, eager to detach themselves from oversight by the state and to keep the role of government in the economy minimal, phrased the rhetoric of their defense in terms of the preservation of private enterprise and stressed the purely private character of the body. They were more likely to do so after the Jacksonian attacks upon privilege emptied connections with the state of much of their value.[17]

The immediate effects were stimulating. At mid-century the corporation in the United States was far more autonomous and was more readily applied to a multitude of business activities than in Europe. General laws made the corporation accessible to any entrepreneur under liberal conditions and contributed to the startling expansion of the economy after 1850.[18]

In the last three decades of the century, however, the severance of its links to the polity seriously hampered the corporation in the effort to organize really large-scale undertakings. In the Old World, where residual connections with the government had survived, existing corporate forms readily accommodated the process of industrial concentration. The giant European combines and cartels appeared with the benevolent approval of the state. But in the United States, the corporation was in no position to seek privilege. As a legal person, it was bound by the limitations that confined other persons. Corporate expansion was subject to the common-law prohibition of restraints upon trade and to the popular disapproval of monopoly, now defined not as a grant by government but as an engrossment of the free market. The arguments in favor of private enterprise now were turned against any action which threatened to limit competition, whether initiated by the state or by individuals.

As a result, many entrepreneurs concerned with an orderly process of concentration at first considered it necessary to act outside the structure of the business corporation through trusts and similar noncorporate forms. These devices bore the odium of conspiracy and were legally and economically hazardous. The resultant tensions at the turn of the century were reflected, on the one hand, in muckraking and trust-busting movements and, on the other, in the businessmen's distrust of government and fear of isolation in a democratic society.

There was a significant parallelism in the development of labor organizations, which after the Civil War also adopted the forms of the voluntary association and, in the absence of recognition by the government, also ran afoul of the fear of conspiracy.[19]

Only after 1890 did creation of the device of the holding company provide easy means for legally acceptable industrial integration. Even then, bitter controversy accompanied every step of the process and left promoters unsure of the permissible limits of concentration. The outcome was a succession of compromises that preserved some degree of fluidity in industrial organization despite a long-term tendency toward concentration. That adjustment has continued to the present, although in an atmosphere much less tense since the end of the First World War.[20]

This pattern of development no doubt had weighty economic consequences. It is plausible to suppose that the flexible institutional arrangements available to business in the United States were somehow connected with the rapid economic growth of the years after 1870. The studies which would demonstrate the nature of that connection remain yet to be written.

After the First World War, the most influential groups of American businessmen relaxed their defensive posture somewhat. The experience of the war revealed that they had little to fear and something to gain from government oversight. The decline of the socialist movement removed a potential threat. And the congenial atmosphere of the 1920's persuaded many that the government could actually further enterprise. Despite the protests of some extremists against the New Deal temper of the 1930's, that confidence did not thereafter waver and, in fact, was strengthened by the events of the 1940's.[21]

In the adjustments of the past half-century, the business corporation has adapted to a wide variety of situations, from that of small individual or family-sized concerns to the great complexes operated by managerial technicians. In all, the key relation is that of voluntary membership through investment in the capital stock.

The strength of the voluntary business association has opened the way to a variety of solutions to particular problems. Mutual savings banks and insurance companies are autonomous of the state and controlled by their own members; yet their officials play a quasi-public role in their relations to the property entrusted to them. Conversely, the public corporation is private in form yet is managed by officers appointed by the government, returning, in some measure, to the original conception of the corporation. Still other needs, as in the case of the telephone, transportation, and power systems, have left the corporation private in both form and control and yet have subjected it to government regulation.[22]

The fact that private property and the profit motive were involved in some cases and not in others was relevant, but not decisive, in shaping the form of organization. More important was the degree to which the voluntary enlistment of support offered an alternative to compulsive action by the state.

Through the nineteenth and twentieth centuries, the line between public and private sectors of society was equally impossible to draw in the noneconomic spheres of life. The history of education, philanthropy, and public health revealed that there was no field preempted entirely by the government; nor was there any, except religion, from which it was entirely excluded. It was never possible clearly to define two distinct spheres: the public, reserved for the state, and the private, for the voluntary association. Politically useful as that distinction may have been, whether for liberal or conservative ends, it had no basis in actual historical development.[23]

Both the voluntary and the coercive forms of action have remained available to Americans, although their relative attractiveness has varied considerably from period to period. Thus, in the past century, reinterpretations of the police and the regulatory functions of the state have led to a steady growth of government activity in education and in matters that once were considered philanthropy. But the very same years witnessed significant extensions of voluntary action into spheres inadequately covered by the state. For example, the widely recognized sense of need for a relief service to meet the emergencies of disaster was filled not by governmental, but by voluntary agencies like the Red Cross.[24]

There have been frequent extensions of voluntary activity into matters generally considered governmental, when immediate conditions made men unwilling to depend upon the state. The inadequacy of established police forces had led to the formation of the vigilante societies of California and of their less well known Eastern predecessors and counterparts. The blurring of the distinction between public and private may also be perceived in the arbitration movement, which attempted to by-pass one of the central functions of government, that of rendering justice.[25]

A variety of efforts at censorship and control by nongovernmental bodies are understandable within the same context. The tyranny of public opinion, often commented on by foreign observers, was an unorganized way of doing what the state could not or would not do. From the point of view of those injured by such pressures, it seemed that anything base and bogus was always labeled American; and patriotism was the duty "to applaud, follow, and obey whatever a ruling clique of newspapers or politicians chooses to say or wants to do." Seen in broader perspective, such pressures were products of the inability of government to affirm accepted standards by coercion.[26] Informal methods of repressing dissent could be as effective as those exercised by the state, as the history of the Union League, the Klan, and the American Protective League revealed.[27]

The inability to use the government for certain types of desired economic control also led to voluntary action to supply the deficiency. Little is known about the early history of trade associations of various sorts although a good deal of attention has been devoted, since the 1930's, to the causes and effects of their restrictive practices. It would be particularly useful to locate the point at which their members turned to the government for aid, as in the efforts to secure and implement fair-trade laws. There are also interesting parallels in the labor movement, both in terms of restrictive practices and of relations to the state.[28]

The complexity of the whole distinction between voluntary and governmental action was most evident when public officials found it necessary or useful to form private associations. Some such bodies were simply social, others professional, and still others had political functions. In some the members joined as individuals, in others by virtue of the position they held. There was inevitably a conflation of roles so that participation in these private bodies may well have affected the exercise of the public office.[29] These associations formed a channel of quasi-governmental communication, influence, and decision outside the recognized political structure. The Association of State Chief Justices could, for instance, criticize the Supreme Court as the tribunals over which they presided could not.

The fluidity of organizational forms, significantly different not only from Europe but also from Canada and Australia, reflects the importance of the function of the voluntary association as an alternative to government action in American life. The hypothesis may be hazarded that fuller examination of the subject will reveal no clear-cut definition of a private sector as the field of voluntary endeavor and of a public sector within which the state operated. Rather, a flexibility of approach was characteristic of the American experience that treated voluntary and state action as alternatives equally available as particular conditions demanded.

More important than any abstract discussion of fields was the changing relation of the member to the association. Unfortunately, little is known of the nature of these developments. The basic forms were the products of a period when associations were small enough to permit an intimacy of membership within which by-laws, rules of procedure, and officers were highly responsive to local idiosyncrasies. In some circumstances that situation still obtains. But growth in the scale and complexity of operations altered many of the fundamental conditions within which the association functioned. In the great industrial corporation, membership has been transformed into the transitory tenure of equities in its stock while the management remains in the hands of a self-perpetuating group of officials. The growth of a bureaucracy with its own character and interests has modified many voluntary philanthropic agencies and has reduced the role of the members to contributors. The appearance of centralized fund-raising bodies like the community funds has further altered the relation; membership in many circumstances has receded in importance and has become little more than the acceptance of an annual tax. The same development has appeared in old, secure trade unions. In churches which recognize a clear distinction between clergy and laymen the tendency has proceeded further with a marked diminution in the competence of the member and an increase in the power of professional functionaries. All these trends have weakened the control of the member and have created kinds of private government with significant powers of coercion. They have also brought into being a bureaucracy with a vested interest in ensuring the survival of the bodies they serve.[30]

Under some circumstances those trends were offset by

loosening conditions of affiliation. In the century after 1840 the decay of small-town life and of older rural forms and the rise of urban centers expanded the individual's capacity to choose which if any associations he would join. Indeed, the image of the unrestrained individual, which in the nineteenth century seemed close to the core of American national identity, emphasized the spontaneous, voluntary qualities of all his affiliations. Characteristically, the tolerance of the atheist or the social rebel as the man who refused to belong, was often a means by which others affirmed that they belonged out of their own free will.

More recent developments, by hardening ethnic lines and encouraging suburban living, have somewhat restricted that latitude of choice. They may have created new problems in the relation of the individual to the association, the consequences of which have yet to unfold.

By widening the range of choices available to the individual, the voluntary association increased his power to act and thus his liberty. It consequently met the needs of personality types for whom a balance between the absence of restraint and the ability to belong was a desirable condition of existence.

The appearance of such personality types can by no means be taken for granted. On the contrary, the desire for a fixed and stable situation that would limit the necessity for choice was at least as usual a condition of human experience. In the European societies in which the migrants to the New World originated, and in many pockets of American population as well, the preference persisted for orderly patterns that would obviate the need for decisions. Individuals, shifting from such environments into situations in which choices were imposed on them, did not always respond to the challenge; they sometimes could do no more than struggle to recreate the forms that would relieve them of the obligation for decision and, if they failed, withdrew into apathy. The circumstances that produced a kind of person eager to make his own choices remain to be explored.[31]

By the middle of the eighteenth century many Americans were no longer disposed to accept institutions or inherited habits simply because they were the products of history, tradition, or the will of superior authorities. By a process which is not yet clear, the transitory character of life in the New World induced them to consider social forms of every sort as the creations of their own wills. They were not born into the church or state, into the community in any of its aspects; they became members by acts of choice. The compulsions that they felt were not those of receiving what existed, but of deciding what they needed to bring into being.

Through the nineteenth century, the constant flow of population into, and within, the country maintained the state of instability. The inability to take anything for granted, the obligation to make choices, was liberating but painful and lay beneath many of the tensions and disorders of American life. It was a condition that stimulated the drive toward voluntary association, a means through which the individual could act and yet do so as the outcome of his will as an individual.

Conversely, the facility with which voluntary organizations were formed undoubtedly had an effect upon American character. The ability to work with others, on his own terms, for the satisfaction of every social want kept the individual from being isolated. There was almost always a range of mediating institutions between the single person and the whole community, so that he did not face the absolute alternatives of withdrawal or conformity. As the power of the state grew, the preservation of some degree of choice was particularly important, for that almost alone warded off the threat of utter personal helplessness.[32]

The voluntary association formed a crucial part of the social environment of Americans. Men for whom freedom meant not simply the absence of irksome limitations but also the extension of their power to act found these organizations doubly useful. The member who joined of his own will and remained free to withdraw did not regard as burdensome, restraints which were accepted spontaneously rather than imposed from without. Yet, in retaining his liberty of affiliation he could still discover the security of identification with groups that set norms and established values by which he guided the conduct of his life.

Thus the voluntary association added to the liberty of the American by extending his power to act. At the cost of the strains involved in making decisions on matters that other men took for granted, he was able to make choices rather than face the brute alternatives of inaction or compulsion by the state. This was an important element in the patterns of freedom that developed in the United States.

The social consequences of voluntarism for the free society of the United States are not readily summarized, for all too few scholars have as yet been occupied in tracing its effects. Two broad tendencies will, no doubt, emerge from any sustained analysis of the data.

Voluntarism, which kept alternative courses of action open, enabled the American economic and social system to recover from the results of mistaken decisions. A study of the nineteenth-century connections between fiscal policy and expansion would reveal that the failure to develop a central bank increased the flexibility of the whole productive system which was, as a result, capable of taking advantage of unexpected opportunities for growth. So too, the spread of railroads after 1830 was not inhibited by the previous commitments of investment in canals and turnpikes. And similar wrong turnings in the development of American education and philanthropy were reversed with relative ease, because alternative modes of action were available to a society which had not totally committed itself to one.[33]

Voluntarism also made possible a high degree of experimentalism. Since no decision was totally binding it was easy to launch off into new and untried directions because the consequences of failure in innovation were not overwhelming. The costs and gains of this experimental, as opposed to a consistently directed or planned, approach are worth intensive investigation. The fact that urban rapid transit was intensively regulated at an early stage may well have had an inhibiting effect upon its development. From the same point of view, it would be worth contrasting the experience of the development of urban housing between 1870 and 1917 when it was entirely free, with the thirty years after 1930 when it became much less so.[34]

There were also heavy social costs to voluntarism. It often entailed waste, inefficiency, and the duplication of efforts. These negative results must certainly be considered in judging whether the play of competitive efforts produced a gain or a loss for the individual and for society.[35]

Most important of all, voluntarism left open the possibility that the members in the emphasis of their individualism would turn inward upon themselves, and would regard the associations to which they belonged as but means of personal self-expression. The unrestrained individualism of the half century after 1870 led many entrepreneurs to lose sight of the functions these organizations were intended to serve, and to use them as means of establishing their own dominance. All too often in this period the business corporation, the university, and philanthropy became narrow, exclusive, and restrictive, heedless of the interests of all but those who controlled them. These attitudes led to a little-noticed but significant crisis in the 1920's, when the prevailing hedonism, individualism, and disregard for the public welfare produced a perceptible decay in the vitality of American voluntary associations.[36]

That condition produced a reaction after 1929 which was among the factors that then led many Americans to turn to the government as the preferable medium for services which were not being adequately supplied through voluntary action.[37]

Paradoxically, since 1930 the voluntary organizations have been stimulated into renewed vitality by the extension of state activity into areas they formerly preempted or dominated. The American system of income and inheritance taxes has encouraged the cumulation of resources in the hands of corporations rather than their dispersal among individuals and has also diverted substantial amounts away from consumption into gifts for philanthropic, cultural, and religious purposes. The awareness that a governmental competitor was ready to assume tasks about the necessity of which there was wide agreement made nongovernmental associations more aware of their responsibilities and set up a yardstick for their performances.

Finally, by relieving the voluntary associations of excessive burdens, the state released their energies for application in other directions. To the extent that governmental bodies took care of the relief of destitution, elementary education, and manipulation of the credit system, voluntary ones extended their activities in other branches of business, social service, and culture. The emergence of the state, whether friendly or hostile, as a powerful factor in labor relations has not curtailed but actually broadened the functions of trade unions.[38]

The capacity to act through noncoercive means remained a critical element in American liberty. It preserved the latitude of choice available to the individual. By sustaining the conviction that desirable ends could be attained without calling upon the state, it helped set limits upon the use of political power without depriving society of services considered essential to its welfare.

The voluntary association, by offering an alternative to the state, was an essential factor in the development of American liberty. The multitude of various subtypes that appeared in the past two centuries differed greatly among themselves, in function, mode of organization, and relations to their members. But they had a common origin and the pattern of their historic evolution left the fate of one kind always interwined with that of the others.

Only a free society was compatible with this wide range of autonomous activities. The necessity for accommodating them forced the government to exercise power loosely and to tolerate collaborative efforts over which it had little control. The ability of men to join in united endeavors for their own purposes was itself hostile to tyranny.

That the voluntary association sometimes served the ends of the state was less important than the fact that it also offered society an alternative to it. By facilitating collective activity of all sorts, freedom of association enabled men to dispense with coercion and also encouraged an active rather than a passive attitude. It was not necessary to wait for the initiative of a higher authority in the face of the need for action; Americans knew how to set themselves going. "This people," wrote Fredrika Bremer in the middle of the nineteenth century, "associate as freely as they breathe." Whenever any subject "arises in society which demands public sympathy or cooperation, a 'Convention' is immediately called to take it into consideration." Life therefore "need never stand still or stagnate. . . . This free association is evidently an organizing and conservative principle of life, called forth to give law and centralization to the floating atoms, to the disintegrated elements." The United States, she concluded, provided at the same time for the highest development of the individual and of the community at large.[39]

☆ VI ☆

RESTRICTIVE
ASSOCIATION

L ACKING as it did the means of coercion, the association
wielded power primarily over its own members whose
ability to withdraw limited its competence even in
relation to them. It had some capacity for coercion but of a
qualified order.

In practice, the loss of the privileges of membership was
itself sometimes a sanction of great importance. Dissidents
might well be frightened if their disobedience led to depriva-
tion of the sacraments of a church or of the protection of a
labor union. The doctor excluded from a medical society was
severely punished if that led to the severance of his connections with hospitals and to the weakening of the confidence
of his patients. The rules of such bodies unquestionably had
some force of compulsion behind them. Yet, however weighty
such penalties might be, they still left the individual with a
margin of choice. Though he suffered through belonging,
that was the price of his own decision to avoid the greater
suffering of not belonging.

The situation changed if some device locked the member
in and prevented him from terminating his affiliation freely.
The situation also changed when the association attempted
to control those who were not members and who did not

of their own will accept its authority. Under either condition the association lost its voluntary character; and that alteration transformed its place in society. It then entered upon an intolerable rivalry with government.

In the past, these conflicts have led to either the destruction or the retreat of the offending group. More generally, subtle barriers have prevented the association from departing too far from its voluntary basis. The association has retained a wide latitude of action, but within the limits of the obligation to respect the interests of its members and of outsiders. The preservation of a delicate line between the freedom of association and the possibility of infringement upon the freedom of individuals has been a necessary condition of American liberty.

Efforts to go beyond that line, to coerce either members or nonmembers, had led to bitter social conflicts, for in the United States the polity was accorded a total monopoly of the use of political power. Such delegations of authority to private organizations as were involved in the N.R.A. were stricken down by the courts with the support of an uneasy public opinion; and it took a long struggle by medical and bar associations to acquire a role in licensing. The early divorce from the state had left the association without legally accepted means of preventing its members from withdrawing or of coercing outsiders.[1]

Any designs therefore to go beyond the recognized limits of what a voluntary body could do, were surreptitious, conducted under the mantle of secrecy and in the form of conspiratorial action. At frequent times and places, impatient men in a free society were impelled to throw off the restraints of voluntarism; as frequently they evoked counterefforts to affirm those restraints without infringing upon the freedom of association.

In the earliest American settlements the lives of every

person and the affairs of every body were open to constant scrutiny by the community. The wide range of offenses of which the courts took cognizance and the requirement for professions of repentance at church meetings revealed the extent to which the individual was obligated to keep his acts unhidden. When Anne Hutchinson resorted to secrecy it was to conceal behavior that transgressed the accepted rules; and her punishment was as much for the surreptitiousness of her meetings as for what went on in them.[2]

As communal controls became laxer in the seventeenth and eighteenth centuries, first in the Southern colonies and then elsewhere, the penalties of unconventionality grew less frightening. Men nevertheless continued to conspire in secrecy, and actually did so more frequently than before. Complex motives impelled them to seek the disguise of concealment.

A variety of secret organizations left evidence of their activity in the years after 1750. The Boston Caucus, the Masonic Order, and the Sons of Liberty were among those which kept their activities at least partly hidden. These groups had in common a defined objective, a sacred oath of loyalty, and a ritual not known to outsiders — features that endowed them all with a conspiratorial quality.[3]

Concealment was, in the first instance, a condition of the unconventional ends at which they aimed. Their members came together because there was no recognized way of achieving what they wished. Since their actions ran counter to either law or custom, external inspection was a source of danger. The attainment of the objective therefore depended upon success in hiding the knowledge of how it was to be pursued.

The whole community generally was aware of the existence of the conspiracy and did not always disapprove of it. Many who did not themselves join might even condone or at least acquiesce in such activities. Secrecy then still served a function for it permitted that to be done in a covert form which men wished to do but from which they were inhibited by rules they nevertheless accepted. Loyal subjects who respected property rights could acquiesce in the flouting of royal authority and the destruction of the East India Company's tea when that was done by unknown Indians. Such an outbreak could be treated as a limited exception which did not threaten the general order.

The disguise of secrecy also protected the conspirators against their own doubts and hesitations. Those who took the decisive step of participation could not simply stifle their inner apprehensions at the prospect of violating firmly fixed conventions. The oath and the ritual, which were a communion with brothers in the band, endowed each individual with a new identity which protected him from the pressure of his own mental reservations. It was therefore possible to do as the new person who was a member of the group what one hesitated to do as the old person hemmed in by a multitude of conflicting loyalties and affiliations.

Secrecy was a potent mechanism. It not only protected the conspirators, but also extended their power over outsiders. The fact that the size and the character of the organization were not precisely known often exaggerated its influence. Since only the members were sure of who belonged, all others had no way of judging the extent of its strength. Its agents might be anywhere; its capacity for discovering, and retaliating against, opposition was undefined and therefore awesome. It was credited or blamed for actions which it did not really initiate; and its operations became a source of anxiety and fear throughout society.

Secrecy gave such bodies unlimited capacity for cooption and exclusion. Only those who were already in could decide who else should be taken in and who barred. In the absence of any public standards of admission, membership was a privilege, often eagerly sought; and the process of selection itself increased the power of the group. The ability to shut applicants out was a means for developing a sense of identification. Those who were in knew themselves — if in no other way, by the fact that they were not out.

Surreptitiousness, in itself, strengthened the awareness of the group's identity and also provided it with an inner discipline. The shared secret was a bond among the participants; and the guilt and danger of sharing it was some assurance that they would obey. The conspiracy was an attractive device not only when there was urgent need for concerted action as among the Sons of Liberty, but also when the primary motive was the intense desire to be chosen as one who belonged, as among the Masons.[4]

After independence and on through the nineteenth century the line between the open association and the secret conspiracy remained vague and tenuous. Americans continued to form clandestine groupings as they formed other organizations. The Order of the Cincinnati, various offshoots of Masonry, a multitude of other lodges and fraternities, and an unclassifiable array of miscellaneous societies satisfied the need for affiliation and for the titles, ritual, and erotic or eccentric behavior not tolerable in their ordinary identities. The grandiloquent designations, the process of robing and disrobing, and the elaborate modes of recognition, in themselves ludicrous or degrading, were dignified by their function in the fraternity. The same forces that encouraged the proliferation of the overt and public bodies also encouraged the spread of the covert and hidden ones.[5]

Some, although not all, of these combinations directed their efforts at specific, definable goals. The gangs that took shape toward the middle of the nineteenth century in the large cities pursued ends that were themselves illegal and were necessarily surreptitious. Other organizations engaged in activities which were not in themselves criminal but which could not so readily be pursued within the public gaze as under cover. So various groups of artisans, journeymen, and other laborers united secretly to improve their rates of remuneration and their working conditions. These organizations grew in scope and size with the development of the economy, reaching a culmination in the Knights of Labor. So, too, later in the century, merchants and manufacturers joined in more limited bodies to control the markets within which they dealt.[6]

At points of crisis, secrecy also became a means of securing power to be used toward ends not attainable by more usual governmental processes. The Republican societies of the 1790's were born of the desire to protect and extend the gains of the Revolution. Between 1854 and 1856, while the nation was torn by the sectional tensions that would soon lead to war, the Order of the Star Spangled Banner mobilized the Know-Nothings in a crusade against the foreign-born. A little more than two decades later, while the South floundered in the uncertainties of reconstruction, the Ku Klux Klan undertook to reduce the freed Negro to a condition of permanent dependence. In the aftermath of the First World War, when a frustrating peace left many Americans in confusion, a new Klan struck out against the minorities held responsible for the inability to return to normalcy. And the depression of the 1930's proved fertile ground for the growth of proto-fascist groups which intended to alter the existing structure of politics.[7]

In all such organizations secrecy transformed accepted modes of association and ultimately aroused the hostility not only of those they threatened but also of much larger numbers of citizens. As the consequences unfolded some of the participants began to seek pretexts for disengaging themselves. That general uneasiness in the face of conspiracy arose from the perception that the compulsion exercised over both members and nonmembers took these bodies beyond the tolerable limits of what a voluntary association could safely do.

The obverse of the desire to be in the group was the fear of being left out of it. All the insiders' rewards of inclusion came at the cost of the outsiders' penalties of exclusion. As a result the appearance of any organization, in which the standards of membership were concealed, was itself a cause of resentment, envy, or outright hostility.

Secrecy tended to transmute those emotions into fear. When the objectives of an association were but vaguely known and its modes of operation were hidden, it became a ready scapegoat for the unexplained ills of a community. Precisely because its influence could not visibly be perceived, it could be discovered everywhere; and activities carried forward in the dark could only be resisted by a total attack upon the whole body. Since its members were sworn to reveal no information, no one could be sure whether a hostile combination existed or not; and in the absence of any kind of evidence, suspicion and anxiety often conjured up imaginary foes in the minds of men who lived under tension. The very idea of a conspiracy repelled Americans who were not in it as much as it attracted those who were.

For a long time the tactics of defense against the secret society were confused by uncertainty about the legal means of limiting its operations. In the sixteenth and seventeenth centuries English law had broadened the concept of conspiracy beyond its earlier limits; a variety of combinations were criminal even though unexecuted and even though not directly related to the administration of justice. A number of statutes then and later also declared specific acts illegal. But it was by no means clear to what extent members were forbidden to do as a group what they could do as individuals.[8]

Nor did the subsequent development of American law provide a reliable guide to action. One line of legislation and decision dealt with combinations of labor. But the early prosecutions of artisans, the cases of Commonwealth *v.* Hunt and of the Danbury Hatters, and the Sherman and Clayton Acts did not seriously affect the ability of workingmen to organize; nor did they create a dependable standard of what was proper and what not.[9]

The law was somewhat more successful in dealing with conspiracies in restraint of trade. The doctrine was clear that price fixing and the division of markets were illegal; and sporadic efforts at enforcement had some success. But the fragmentary quality in every American confrontation of the problem revealed the uncertainty here too in drawing the line between freedom of enterprise and the conspiratorial violation of the freedom of others.[10]

Outside these areas was territory that long remained altogether uncharted. The right of association was so firmly embedded in American society that there seemed no desirable means of asking government to circumscribe it. Not until after the First World War did measures against criminal syndicalism and later against subversive organizations move significantly in this direction. Even these steps relied more upon the seditious than upon the conspiratorial nature of the offenses. Through most of American history, it was futile to seek the protection of the law against the power of the secret organization.[11]

That heightened the dread of the conspiracy, real or fancied. Since the forces at work were not clearly known and since there was no readily available instrument for resisting them, they evoked panicky countermovements. Trepidations about what might be going on sometimes called such movements into existence, with little or no foundation in fact. Thus, from the early eighteenth century onward, rumors of slave conspiracies again and again caused explosive reactions among whites. Similarly, in the uncertainty of the first decades of the Republic's life, some groups fastened their anxiety upon the aristocratic designs of the Cincinnati, while others found causes for concern in the plots of the Jacobins and illuminati.[12]

The nineteenth century was enlivened with a succession of discoveries of secret conspiracies against the liberties of the people. For a time, the suspicious citizens were most likely to be the members of the orthodox churches disturbed by the nonconformity of some of their neighbors. The Masons, the Mormons, the Catholics, and the Jews each in turn became the object of repressive organizations which imagined that they were uncovering evidence of surreptitious, or at least different and therefore dubious, activities. Such hostile movements challenged not only the principles of freedom of association but also those of religious freedom.

Later in the century, the Americans most sensitive to the fear of conspiracy were those resolved to defend a social order threatened by rapid change. The Populist Manifesto of 1895 exposed a plot formed "as early as 1865–66 . . . between the gold gamblers of Europe and America to . . . fasten upon the country the single gold standard of Britain." The international bankers, the wild-eyed populists, the anarchists, the brewers, and, still later, the Communists were regarded as agents of hostile powers, intent upon destroying the liberties of the Republic. Constant vigilance and the most vigorous retaliatory measures were necessary in self-defense.[13]

The efforts to resist conspiracy found expression in a variety of forms. The size and structure of the resultant organization, the duration of the fear, and the intensity of the emotions generated varied from situation to situation. The provocation might be real, fancied, or exaggerated; and the response might erupt into violent action or dissipate itself in emotional rhetoric. Whatever the case, all such movements had in common a distinctive posture of self-defense against forces which legitimate means could not control. Whether it was because the threat seemed to be international in character or because its ramifications were considered unusually extensive, these were extraordinary reactions to crises not manageable by the usual instruments of society.

That was why anticonspiratorial movements sometimes themselves became conspiracies. The will to resist the illicit activities of the others was a bond that identified and united the group. The secret lodges of the Know-Nothings were the means of combating the secret designs of the Catholics; and the second Klan fought the Elders of Zion. Being "anti" was in itself a step toward belonging.

Despite the readiness with which Americans slipped into secret associations, the damage to society was relatively slight. Only in the case of the Klan during Reconstruction can one find demonstrable permanent effects; and that outbreak was so imbedded in a complex pattern of other forces working in the same direction that it is difficult to delimit its precise influence. More generally, these activities led to limited, local outbursts of passion and to conflicts of a transitory nature. In fact, they sometimes had a cathartic effect, in which the outburst of pent-up hatreds and fears relieved men of anxieties that had remained troublesome while concealed. Such release often cleared the air and left the way open for more constructive resolution of underlying difficulties.

Neither conspiracy nor counterconspiracy was able to seize power or long to exercise control even in a limited section of the country. There was no parallel here to the Mafia of Sicily or the *Broederbond* of the Union of South Africa. Nor did the machinery of American government fall into the hands of the Fascists or Communists as happened in central and eastern Europe. The ability to contain such threats within a very restricted scope was an early and continuing element in the preservation of liberty in the United States.[14]

The federalism of American society and its respect for constitutional procedures and rights created a counterweight to all such extraordinary attempts to grasp power. In addition, institutional flexibility permitted the nation to absorb the shock of various secret combinations without permanent damaging effects. The history of anti-Masonry provides a striking illustration. That movement took form in a period of widespread discontent with the existing arrangements for selecting political officeholders. The anti-Masons gained considerable strength, for a time, by attracting all sorts of aggrieved men who believed they were not properly represented in the government. Although suspicion of the Masons persisted on until the end of the nineteenth century, the organized anti-Masonic movement faded and lost significance when the development of the political parties of the 1830's offered an alternative and better recognized means of achieving the same end. The new parties destroyed the power of the old caucuses and brought the whole process of nomination out into the open, cutting the ground out from under anti-Masonry.[15] Likewise, the proto-Fascism that developed in the 1930's was emptied of much of its capacity for damage by the changes introduced by the New Deal which diverted popular discontent into other channels.[16]

As important, the great social diversity of the nation made it difficult for a conspiracy to take hold by bringing within its sway sufficiently large numbers to form a basis for permanent control. The experience of the Know-Nothings between 1854 and 1856 was instructive. The movement gained power as long as it could simply focus on hostility to the foreign-born. When its members tried to achieve a positive national program, they quickly discovered that their points of view were different and irreconcilable. The New England Know-Nothings who were anti-immigrant because the Irish were tolerant of slavery could not meet together with the Southern Know-Nothings who were anti-immigrant because the Germans were hostile to slavery. And neither of these groups had much in common with the Know-Nothings of the middle states who wished to evade the whole slavery question. As soon as the movement ceased to be local, it fell apart.

Again, the proto-Fascist movements of the 1930's were split among so many factions fundamentally incompatible with one another that they never arrived at a basis for cooperation. In a nation divided among numerous different sectional, economic, ethnic, and cultural groups a conspiracy which depended upon homogeneity could only enlist the support of small minorities and was limited in its capacity to do harm. The social structure of the United States as well as its institutions of government were a means of containing and limiting the effects of conspiracy, both to preserve the liberty of association and to prevent abuses of it.[17]

The kind of "private government" that associations exercised over their members and the influence they exerted over others remained important. But, such power as that brought them was circumscribed by the limits of possible social disapproval, of potential counteraction, and of the threat of public control. The association that moved beyond the tolerable boundaries faced the risk of damaging retaliation.

It was therefore imperative that a group which wished to act without the fear of drawing undesirable consequences upon itself should do so in ways that would make clear that it was not a conspiracy. Secrecy was "the shield of sin."[18] Motives that were pure were also visible. Every association had an obligation to make public its objectives and its modes of operation. Only in this way could it escape the odium of suspicion. The trade associations against which so much animus was earlier directed took on a much more innocent appearance when they emerged into the open after 1912.[19]

Furthermore, organized groups had to avoid such flagrant abuses of their power as might evoke an outcry either from their own members or from others affected by their actions. That is, they had to conduct their affairs according to standards that the community generally considered reasonable. Otherwise they stirred up hostility and, after the enactment of the Fourteenth Amendment, might face judicial proceedings.

Suspended over the associations was always the possibility of regulation by the government. Those which had an impact upon only a few individuals were not likely to attract the attention of the state. But those whose influence was consequential had to bear in mind the eventuality that people adversely affected by its actions might seek recourse in the courts or in the legislature, which had ample means for protecting the individual against violations of his rights without due process.

In a purely negative sense, the government could refuse to provide the means of coercion for carrying out the wishes of groups that acted against public policy. Upon such grounds, for instance, the Supreme Court in 1948 struck down the possibility of enforcing restrictive covenants in housing.[20] But the courts were able to go even farther and to hold that some actions of private associations had inherent in them a public interest that made them susceptible to control. Thus, although political parties were originally considered extra-governmental, the white primary and even the preprimary elections of private associations were held to violate the rights of the Negroes excluded from them.[21]

The situation was clearer still when an association derived some of its power from the government, for it was presumed that all such grants were directed toward a public end. A transportation or broadcasting company which operated through a franchise, by its very acceptance of the privilege implicitly recognized the obligation to provide equal services to those who would use it. A labor union which attained its position through the protection of the law had responsibilities for using reasonable standards of selection in admitting or rejecting candidates; and the law regulated many of its internal affairs to protect the rights of its members. A corporation that accepted public favors in building a housing project, by virtue thereof also accepted the obligation to treat prospective tenants equally. Such bodies became to some extent "repositories of official power" and were obliged to act "in submission to the mandates of equality and liberty" that bound officials everywhere.[22]

There remained a frontier zone in which rights and duties were not fully or precisely defined, at least by the courts. Did the agreement on the part of a privately constituted group to boycott a book or a motion picture constitute censorship? How much privilege did a housing development have to accept to become endowed with the public attributes that made racial discrimination illegal in it? To draw the line in such matters was not easy. But that a line existed beyond which the affairs of private associations were susceptible to public control was rarely questioned.[23]

The potential for regulation and oversight did not seriously curtail the ability of the association to act. Indeed, by marking out the limits within which its operations were proper, it may well have strengthened them. In any case it helped to maintain a balance among the varieties of choices that remained open to the individual.

There remains to be considered the possibility that associations might infringe upon the liberty of their members and others, not through use of governmental power nor through secrecy, but through the informal but binding compulsions of kinship. Conceivably the ethnic groups that played so important a part in American life might have extended the power of their constituent organizations by alienating the individual from the rest of society. The Japanese or Yankee or Jew who had contacts only within his own group became utterly dependent upon it and thereby lost some freedom of choice. Under such conditions the penalty of exclusion from the church or the lodge was unbearable.

In the United States, however, there were significant social limits upon the ability of various groups entirely to segregate themselves. Those limits conditioned the kinds of control ethnic associations exercised. The distances between the various elements of the population were rarely so great as to make ostracism a decisive threat.

Only in a few cases did an ethnic group achieve isolation in an enclave of its own. The Amish of Pennsylvania and, occasionally, other sects, for generation after generation maintained their seclusion from the dominant currents of American society. Yet these examples were clearly exceptional and influenced small numbers only. There was no counterpart here of such separateness as the French Canadians of Quebec maintained for a long time.[24]

American ethnic groups maintained their fluidity through a delicate balance between the forces that detached and those that connected their members to the rest of the society. They preserved their identity without becoming segregated or isolated enclaves in the total society. Functioning effectively over long periods, they nevertheless were inhibited from acquiring attributes that would permanently and decisively set apart the individuals affiliated with them. The balance left room for wide areas of personal choice on the part of the members to whose interests and ideas the group was necessarily sensitive.

Deprived of means of compulsion, the ethnic group would have retained only a limited capacity to discipline; individuals could, if they wished, bear its penalties without inordinate suffering because their lives were not totally encompassed within its borders. They were not entirely isolated from the rest of the society; alternatives remained open.

It was significant in preventing that isolation that American governmental institutions recognized individuals, not groups.[25] All the rights and privileges of citizenship and all the guarantees of participation in society adhered to persons, not to larger entities; even the corporation had to find shelter behind the fiction of legal personality. No collectivity could entrench itself between the individual and the goals he wished to attain.

Furthermore, the internal dynamics of many groups led them to seek, at the same time, to preserve their own identity and yet to reach out to convert and absorb outsiders. These contradictory impulses were particularly characteristic of, although by no means confined to, those of English descent who felt a special compulsion to make their limits coextensive with the whole nation.

By the eighteenth century, a missionary spirit had dissolved the earlier exclusive sense of election that had separated one element from another. The desire to bar outsiders gave way to an urge to assimilate them; and a variety of groups came to consider themselves in competition for new adherents. The appearance of new religious sects which conducted unremitting raids upon the unaffiliated or loosely affiliated thereafter stimulated the rivalry for loyalty.[26]

The strand of millenarianism that ran through much of the activity of some of the ethnic groups added force to their expansive tendency. The inclination to break with the past and the present, to place one's hopes in an order still to be created rather than in one that was inherited, added to the urgency to increase the membership of the body that knew the way to reform. It also minimized the importance of antecedents.[27]

The ability to make converts, either religious or social, demanded some accommodation to the tastes, interests, and ideas of those who were to be persuaded. Outsiders could not be compelled to come in; they had to be convinced to do so voluntarily. And no group could attract them by stressing the unique qualities of its own inheritance. A subtle process of adjustment found each group dirfting away from the particularities of its heritage and reaching out toward a more general view of its place in the whole society.

The desire to assimilate outsiders altered many ethnic organizations. Quaker attitudes of benevolence, originally confined within the group, acquired a universal character when the Friends recognized their obligations to their neighbors. Institutions for higher education established to serve a specific ethnic element also changed as they expanded their appeal. The early sectarian colleges were thus driven steadily to broaden their social bases.[28]

The competition for membership also affected those groups which had no clear missionary intentions. The Jews and Italians of 1900, for instance, did not aim to draw the other American into their fold, but simply wished to preserve their hold over their own adherents. They could not depend on external support to do so for the law recognized the right of any group to seek converts. Even those which were not aggressive had to offset the attractions of potential rivals by establishing their own images as completely American and by emphasizing the depth of their own roots in the country. They developed a capacity for resisting the incursion of other groups only by diminishing the range of differences that set them apart. To retain the loyalty of the second generation the Italians and the Jews had to shed their peculiarities of behavior and belief and to emphasize their Americanism. The necessities of coexistence in the open society prevented any segment of the population from erecting insurmountable walls about itself.[29]

The situation remained open because some contact among the members of various groups was inescapable. The organization of American economic, political, and cultural life compelled individuals often to disregard ethnic lines. The productive system, for instance, did not tolerate the development of caste-like strata. In the swiftly expanding competitive order success held a preeminent value and the dangers of catastrophic failure were always imminent; men could not afford to subordinate the calculations of the market place to noneconomic considerations. The entrepreneur, aware of his own interests, hired the most efficient hand, bought from the cheapest seller, sold to the highest bidder, or suffered in consequence. So, too, no group formed a majority secure enough to hold political power except on a very local level; those who sought office or advantages through politics were compelled to develop alliances that transcended ethnic divisions. Finally, the press, the radio, and the other media for general communication addressed individuals rather than members of groups. Even when a given newspaper began with a specific ethnic orientation, the advantages of reaching out for the largest possible audience transformed those which survived and expanded. In this area too, American society remained open and its fluidity prevented any group from maintaining its exclusiveness for very long.

The imperatives of an open society weighed heavily against the prospect that an individual could confine himself within the limits of a narrow group. Much as he sought the security of belonging and cherished the values of being an insider, there were points at which his chances in life depended upon the ability to move outside the ethnic limits. The extent of the opportunities for social mobility was an extremely important factor in maintaining or diminishing the exclusiveness of these groupings. Although we do not yet possess more than a rudimentary knowledge of the way in which the processes of social mobility worked, there is sufficient indication that movement and the belief in its feasibility were genuine enough to inhibit complete isolation.[30]

Only when the opportunities for social mobility seemed to narrow did underprivileged ethnic groups withdraw from unrewarding and painful contacts with outsiders. The Negroes, disappointed by the results of emancipation and rejected by the racism of the whites; the Chinese and Japanese, segregated by their color; and the Jews and other new immigrants of the 1890's who confronted imposing discriminatory barriers—for greater or lesser periods were thrown back into their own societies. But, when external hostility abated and the range of permitted contacts widened, then their dependence upon fellowship with their own kind eased.[31]

So long as American society remained open and fluid freedom of association did not permit an ethnic group to impose excessive restraints upon its own members. The organizations formed within these limits operated inside a range prescribed by their ability to elicit the loyalty and consent of those who belonged to them.

The pattern of institutional forces that usually kept the impulse toward association from becoming oppressive extended the ability of the individual to make choices and increased his power to act. The group rarely proved effective as an instrument of restraint although men were often tempted to use it as such by the communal and personal forces that drew them into it. Constant vigilance against conspiratorial tendencies and a social order that loosened ethnic ties limited the coercive capacity of the association. Without the support of the political force of which the government was sole custodian, none could rule except through the assent of its members. Thus far no such group has long been able to enlist such support; and voluntary associations have operated effectively to increase rather than to contract the liberty of the individual.

The danger of restrictive conspiracy was a concomitant of

freedom of association. A tyrant who forbade all groups he did not control faced no problem of decision as to which were legitimate and which were not. A society that could determine what the common weal was could tolerate those which furthered the common weal and proscribe others which did not.

But when, as in the United States, neither the government nor any authoritative body had the power to determine what the common weal was, there was no firm standard of judgment. Every grouping of men operated autonomously. Hence the risk that any one of them might invade the rights of others. Statutory restraints, prosecutions by the state, the glare of publicity, the threats of regulation and retaliatory counterassociations limited the danger. But the ultimate bulwark against conspiratorial movements was their need to retain the loyalty and consent of their own members who had other, more comprehensive interests in the social order. The individuals whose support was essential, until now have not fully yielded it. Awareness that their fate was not bound in with that of a single narrow group, and a multitude of affiliations with other associations induced them to withdraw before the conspiracy could succeed.

☆VII☆
POWER AND
THE WEALTH
OF MEN

AMERICANS judged the voluntary association, as they judged the state, by the criterion of the ends to be served. Just as the coercive power of government was contained within procedures and limits defined in the light of the goals of the society, so the activities of any groups were circumscribed by the general acceptability of their purpose.

The conception of the proper end of social action at any given point in history must be inferred from scattered utterances and fragmentary measures; for a whole view was rarely formulated and expressed except in such vague terms as "furtherance of the general welfare." Yet an underlying consciousness of common purpose did exist and was kept alive by many elements in the American situation.[1]

In actuality, the population included a variety of disparate types. Planters and slaves, factory owners and farmers, miners and merchants formed distinct strata in the society; and the lines that separated them, while less rigid at some times than at others, were always there. The motives that moved these men as individuals and the interests that swayed them as groups were by no means always identical and were often contradictory. Since none was in a position arbitrarily to impose its will upon all the others, it remained necessary to formulate, explain, and justify particular objectives in terms of general goals attractive to the whole society.

Among the wide range of ends toward which Americans have been permissive, one has stood preeminent in the consistency of its general acceptance. The use of coercive power by the polity or of influence by association has most readily been recognized as valid when it tended to increase the wealth of the whole society, however that was defined. Other values have generally been subordinated to, or interpreted in terms of, this one.

Perhaps because settlement in the New World was long precarious, and dependent upon promotional activity that could only be sustained through the continuing proof of productivity, Americans were sensitive to the pressure of proving their ability to create wealth. Even the Puritans, dedicated as they were to the goal of exemplifying holiness on earth, early came to interpret prosperity as a measure of their ability to please God. Steps that added to the total store of goods were desirable as evidence of divine favor toward the community, just as the individual's acquisition of riches was a sign of his progress toward salvation.[2]

Later, the persistence of frontier conditions, the apparent abundance of the continent thrown open to the advance of thousands of new families, and the growing conviction that the material universe was utterly malleable in the hands of man confirmed the tendency to interpret social goals in terms of the creation of wealth. Still later, the successive thrusts of immigrant populations into the land of opportunity, the new horizons revealed by industrialization and science, and the confidence engendered by seemingly limitless expansion further strengthened the tendency. The release of energy toward productive ends has thus been a constant factor in terms of which Americans have interpreted their freedom. They were willing to consent to the acts of governments and

associations which promised to increase the store of resources, for the well-being of each individual seemed to turn
upon doing so.[3]

The growth of wealth was at first viewed absolutely and
measured by the total of goods available to the whole society. So long as the community was whole, integrated, and
homogeneous, the overriding consideration among its members was the extent of its common possessions, for the welfare of each was bound in with the welfare of all.[4]

As the community began to fall into fragments soon after
settlement, the conception of wealth tended to become in-
dividualized. By the mid-eighteenth century, welfare came
to be viewed in personal rather than social terms. The element of selfish calculation had never been absent from decisions on the numerous issues that divided men; but it had
earlier been subordinate to, or at least couched in terms of,
the larger good. Now each person was more likely to form his
judgments in terms of a prosperity abstracted from that of
the group of which he was a part. The change was an aspect
of a general process which by the time of the Great Awaken-
ing also redefined virtue in an individual rather than in a
communal context and by the second half of the century
altered the ways of regarding property, weakening the emphasis upon its social use and strengthening that upon the
personal right to it.[5]

The idea of the commonwealth, of a state with an interest
which transcended those of its component members, endured
on into the nineteenth century, although it corresponded less
than ever before to a social order in which diverse elements
contended with one another. The gradual adjustments to the
pressures of the real divisions within the country in time wore
away the commonwealth conception; and thereafter the
wealth of the nation was regarded as the sum of the wealth
of the particular individuals aggregated in it.[6]

In the economy of the nineteenth century each man struggled toward the attainment of his own good, in the faith that

a self-regulating competitive mechanism would assure the service of the good of all. But that faith itself required evidence; it was sustained by the widespread diffusion of the output of the productive system and by the opportunities open to men to make what they could of their talents, capital, and willingness to run risks. Whatever formal terms might measure the total yield or gross national product, the individual's standard of judgment remained the extent to which rewards were accessible to him. Without any overarching conception of the community as a whole, he now determined whether power was used to advance his liberty or not by the degree to which it widened or narrowed his opportunities.[7]

Hence the significance of social mobility in American history. The possession of a stake in society or of an opportunity to acquire one was the pivot upon which the representative republican polity turned, for it supplied assurance that men would consent to be governed. In the long argument over the nature of the American state that extended from the constitutional debates of the 1780's to the controversy beween John Adams and John Taylor in 1814, the element that permitted an accommodation of opposing views was the belief that wealth would "be considerably distributed, to sustain a democratick republick."[8]

In the early nineteenth century, free land and free enterprise kept the goods produced by the society within the reach of all. Daniel Webster celebrated the virtues of an order that made every competent man a landed yeoman; and Edward Everett, pointing to the fluidity of business, explained, "the wheel of fortune is in constant operation, and the poor in one generation furnish the rich of the next."[9]

By the end of the century that conviction was more difficult to maintain. The appearance of great concentrations of wealth in the hands of a few was not so troubling as was the development of a depressed group of hopeless laborers. "In proportion as the working men feel the impassibility of the gulf that separates them from the rich class, they tend to become discontented and disaffected; and . . . the chances of the average poor man to acquire wealth becomes smaller, thus putting him among the protestants against the existing situation." Beneath the expressed fears of proletarians, foreigners, Negroes, anarchists, Populists, "agitators," and Wobblies was the perception that the number of men was growing who might not consent to be governed.[10]

The expressed creed of the society continued to affirm the possibility of individual achievement through self-enrichment. Americans accepted the assurance of Russell Conwell "that the opportunity to get rich . . . is within the reach of almost every man"; and that there was "not a poor person in the United States who was not made poor by his own shortcomings." The belief was necessary, for the underlying premise of the conception that power might properly be used to increase the wealth of the community was the assumption that wealth so maximized would be accessible to all. This was the basic meaning of the American idea of equality of opportunity.[11]

It is not at all clear, however, whether the idea that the opportunity to get rich was available to all, conformed to reality and to what extent it did so. It may be posited as a working hypothesis that most of the difficulties in defining liberty that arose in the purely political sphere in the United States were eased by the underlying fluidity of the social structure which in turn was derived from a relatively high rate of social mobility. Proof is not yet available. Plausible as these statements seem, the evidence to validate or refute them has not yet been collected or analyzed.

The history of social mobility has heretofore received no study whatever. Historians have taken for granted the fluidity of American society and have often ascribed to it a uniqueness as compared with other societies; but they have done so on the basis of general impressions rather than of systematically organized data. The sociologists who have more usually dealt with this question have not treated it across any extended time interval and their conclusions have therefore necessarily been limited.

Recent contemporary investigations have suggested that the extent and rate of American mobility have popularly been exaggerated, and have also cast doubt on the degree of difference that obtained between the United States and other countries. All societies have permitted some reshuffling among their members; and structural economic and social changes in the last two centuries have everywhere accelerated the rate.[12] Without more knowledge in chronological depth than we now possess it is hard to draw meaningful inferences from these suggestions. They could, conceivably, indicate either that mobility in the United States was more rapid in earlier periods and has now slackened or that there never was a consequential deviation by this country from the pattern of development in other societies.

There is a third line of approach to the problem. The failure to perceive significant differences between the situation in the United States and that in Europe or Asia may be the product of inadequacies in current sociological conceptions and methods of measurement. The conclusions of many generations of observers cannot simply be written off as biased or ignorant. The vast array of political and social materials which suggest that society was more fluid in America than elsewhere must be accounted for. Either there was a persistent distortion in the angle of vision of all these observers; or the contemporary sociological data is faulty; or the present mode of examining and assessing the phenomena thrown together as social mobility is deceptive; or the fluidity of a society is independent of the rate of social mobility, the capacity of some individuals to move from one rank to another being but slightly affected by the rigidity of the lines among them. All these possibilities need exploration.[13]

The poor quality of available historical information impedes the study of the general course of American social mobility. The uncertainty of registration data, the inability to trace individuals from census to census, and a complex of factors related to the migration of the population make it impossible reliably to trace either the career lines of large groups of individuals or significant intergenerational changes. A sustained effort is needed to compensate for the absence of governmental data by finding information on family employments over relatively long periods.[14]

However useful such investigations will prove, other lines of analysis will also be pursued. It may be a mistake to study social mobility in the gross as if it were a uniform process in which all movements from one occupational or status level to another were of equal importance. In the last two hundred years rapid economic change in every society has produced a high degree of spatial and occupational movement. Industrialization and urbanization have everywhere created a demand for factory and white-collar labor which could only be satisfied by recruitment from new sources. Yet not all such shifts of population had the same meaning. Peasants who moved to a city to become proletarians were certainly mobile socially. Their children who filled the large number of clerical and sales positions created by economic development would also register as mobile by the usual measurements. One could therefore expect everywhere to find large shifts from rural to urban, from "manual" to "nonmanual" callings.

But the consequences for the structure of society varied strikingly from place to place. Such intergenerational mobility may very well have been as characteristic of Japan in the first quarter of the twentieth century as of the United States. But the one society was far more stratified than the other.

Furthermore, social mobility, as many students have measured it, is not the only significant index of change in status. An apprentice who completed his term in 1820 might still be practicing his handicraft in 1860, yet have suffered a genuine decline in status through the operation of external economic forces. Conversely, the auto worker or coal miner climbed rapidly between 1930 and 1960, without a change in occupation.

What is necessary is not only a study of mobility as a general phenomonon, but also an examination of particular aspects of the relation between occupations, opportunity, and wealth, on the one hand, and the political and cultural components of power and freedom, on the other. Such an approach will add more useful insights into the degree of fluidity in American society to supplement those derived from broad comprehensive analyses of occupational shifts.

These relations may be examined both through studies of particular communities and through the systematic analysis of the general factors that influenced the structure of society. The wide variety of urban types in the United States, the relative recency of settlement in many places, and the great size of some cities complicate the tasks of analysis and render hazardous generalizations based upon the experience of particular communities. It will be profitable to examine a number of representative examples of varying sizes, tracing them through the initial phases of their growth until they displayed some degree of stability. Within these cities one could investigate concretely the operations of the economic, social, and cultural determinants of status. It will often be advantageous to select for study, places for which data from contemporary surveys can be compared with that drawn from historical sources.[15]

There will remain a wide variety of materials that will yield only to more comprehensive treatment independently of the framework of the individual community. These may be ordered through an investigation of the forces and institutional determinants that tended to ease or retard the ability of individuals to move a significant distance from one social

level to another. The role of the government, the character
of the educational system, the distribution of property, and
the complexity of the social order were all relevant, although
the precise nature of the relation involved is by no means
clear.

The ability to move about the country freely satisfied one
of the conditions of social mobility. The relative emptiness of
the continent for a long time, the early breakdown of residence requirements, the rapid pace of expansion, and the
frequent shifts in the location of industry encouraged fluidity
in settlement. In addition, the weakness of communal ties
and individual rootlessness permitted men to shift their families about to where opportunities were most attractive. The
ease with which the population was constantly being redis-
tributed acquired its significance from the social context.
The process of migration offered the the occasion for a reshuffling of status, for new beginnings outside inherited institutions. It opened to some the possibility of rising and exposed others to the danger of falling.

The factors that shaped the social context were complex.
Efforts by the state to restrict access to the occupation of an
individual's choice were never important in the United
States. In the seventeenth century such restrictions were
usual in the Europe from which the colonists migrated; and
they survived across the Atlantic on into the nineteenth century. Yet in the United States attempts to limit the admission
to any calling through government licensing generally failed
entirely or succeeded only under very special circumstances.
Neither provincial nor municipal controls were firm enough
to put any branch of commerce out of the reach of ambitious
entrepreneurs although special monopolies, as in the fur
trade, were feasible for short periods. Efforts to license the
handicrafts were as futile as those to restrain trade. With the
decay of communal conceptions of wealth and property and

later with the disappearance of the Commonwealth idea, the very basis for such state action collapsed, not to be restored until licensing was to be reinterpreted as a form of police regulation. The trend toward liberality was, no doubt, related to the developing attitudes toward monopolies and to the peculiar evolution of the professions. In any case, the failure to establish and maintain a rigid system of licensing in practice generally removed a potential drag upon social mobility in the United States.[16]

The development of the American educational system in the long run positively accelerated social mobility. The schools imparted to their students a set of values that were goads in the struggle for success; they supplied an alternative, of ever-growing importance, to the intergenerational or family succession to certain occupations.[17] Yet their precise role was by no means clear.

The connection between the schools and social mobility did not arise from their ability to equip the student with the specific skills of desirable careers. It was true that a mercantile society, and, even more so, an industrial one, required the services of men and women who could read and write, calculate, read blueprints, and follow the instructions necessary to operate complex machines. The preparation of the hands and minds needed for such tasks did not, itself, stimulate mobility. Indeed, it is more than likely that people trained for such particular jobs would be drawn from, and would remain in, the social strata already close to them.

The relation of the school to social mobility was more complex. The first significant changes in educational patterns in the colonies came in the late seventeenth century with the decay of apprenticeship. The old forms of craft training continued to decline thereafter in the context of radical shifts in the character of family and community organization.[18] Neither then nor later did the organized school system assume the task of instruction in particular vocational skills.

On into the nineteenth century the grammar and primary schools, the academies and high schools, and the colleges explicitly disavowed the intention of preparing youths for specific jobs as apprenticeship had done. Vocational education tended to develop outside the formal educational arrangements; and when it did intrude into the recognized curriculum, it took a subordinate position of low esteem and applied primarily to the less desirable types of jobs. In callings that ranked high, such as medicine, law, and business, apprenticeship — even when it followed a college education — remained the predominant mode of preparation until almost the end of the nineteenth century.[19]

It is possible that the connection of the schools with social mobility lay in their ability to provide the student with generalized skills and attitudes which did not ready him for any specific employment, but did enable him to move from one to another, capitalizing upon opportunities as they turned up. The fact that the educational system was long only loosely articulated and never rigidly controlled by a central authority enabled individuals to enter it at varying points in their careers, to find second chances and to recoup from mistakes or wrong decisions. This is an attractive hypothesis. But it would have to be sustained both by an analysis of curricula and by an examination of sample career lines to discover a link between crucial moves and what had happened in the schools.[20]

Or, alternatively, it may be that the connection with social mobility lay not in what the schools did, but in who their students were. The educational system moved only slowly to accommodate a substantial percentage of all children. Until the twentieth century, whatever channels of advancement they opened up were available only to limited segments of the population. It is difficult as yet to estimate their influence upon social mobility. Only by understanding the factors involved in the recruitment of the student body can one judge whether the educational apparatus was itself important in creating access to good positions, or whether it simply seemed important because the types of students who used it moved into careers they would have taken up in any case. Did the high school of the 1890's, for instance, increase the career chances of the boys who graduated from it, or were only such likely to attend as were already assured advancement by strategic family or ethnic connections? Such questions are intimately related to the problems raised by the desire of various groups, from time to time, to use the schools as devices of exclusion, beyond the normal degree of selectivity in such institutions.[21]

In examining these alternative hypotheses it will be useful to focus upon those critical periods when the schools, at one level or another, opened their doors to new social groups. The rapid spread of colleges in the mid-eighteenth century and in the first quarter of the nineteenth century, the development of public elementary education toward mid-century, and the broadened clientele of the high schools after 1918, offer strategic opportunities for assessing the effects of education as a factor influencing the rate of social mobility.[22]

The effects of changes in education were bound in with the economic context in which they occurred. It has been all too easy to assume a relation between the lack of rigid stratification and the widespread diffusion of property among all but the very underprivileged in the United States. More important is the task of defining that relation precisely.

There has, for instance, been a long and largely fruitless controversy among historians over the safety-valve theory. Some, particularly the followers of Frederick Jackson Turner, have ascribed to the availability of empty land and to the liberal federal and state land systems a determining influence upon the mobility of labor which, in turn, eased discontent and inhibited the development of vigorous protest movements. Others have denied that the connection existed and have emphasized the relative paucity of the number of industrial workers who became farmers and the relative insignficance of the land given away through homesteading.[23]

Both positions are tenable, although neither is adequate. Neither takes account of the full range of influences that dispersed property among various sectors of the American population. The availability of land was but one of these. Alienated under political conditions which prevented the concentration of holdings and the collective enterprises that appeared on other frontiers, the open acres of the West supplied an outlet for the kinds of farmers and artisans who in eighteenth-and nineteenth-century Europe were depressed into the ranks of the industrial proletariat.[24]

The dominant patterns of inheritance also tended to disperse landed wealth. Primogeniture and entail had all but disappeared even before revolutionary legislation wiped them out; such practices were not as important in an empty continent where labor was scarce, as they had been in England. More consequential, the most prevalent practices in the bequeathal of estates preserved the individual holdings at a viable size. There was no parallel here to the process of morcellation that complicated the lives of German and Irish peasants. Despite unfavorable economic conditions, farming continued to open opportunities to those who wished to enter it. Even the development of tenantry late in the nineteenth century was sometimes a means of stimulating mobility.[25]

The expansion of the productive system also encouraged the diffusion of other forms of property among those groups which sought to advance through various types of entrepreneurial activity. The recent diffusion among many elements in the population of holding of investment securities, although not as widespread as is sometimes supposed, gave a stake in the economy to ever-broader sections of the population. That tendency was related to the development of capital markets and of stock speculation and to the evolution of the corporation. It may also reflect the effects of life insurance practice. More important still, it may have depended for a long time upon the inability of rigid institutions to reduce the amount available by laying a dead hand upon property. The holdings of churches, schools, and charities were relatively small and fluid as long as they depended primarily upon voluntary contributions to finance their expenditures. It remains to be seen when the recent growth of the capital in the hands of such bodies will appreciably alter the situation.[26]

The widespread diffusion of property has given a great many Americans access to disposable capital. The proportion who were potential entrepreneurs was unusually large in comparison with other societies. Recent interpretations which minimize the differences between the United States and Europe are not altogether convincing for they focus primarily on the derivation of big business leadership in a rather unusual period. The recent development of a corps of managers, not owners of the capital they use, may well have created an exceptional situation, not representative of American experience in the past.[27]

More to the point in any effort to understand the relation of business to social mobility would be a serious examination of the patterns of petty trade and retailing, especially in the nineteenth century. Small-town trade, even after it became vulnerable to competition from the chain store and the mail-order house, long offered a means to advancement through the independent employment of capital. The westward movement which generated new towns at each shift of the line of settlement also expanded the chances for enterprise. The effects upon retailing of the growth of metropolitan markets may have contracted those opportunities somewhat in the twentieth century, but they have hardly disappeared entirely. When we know more about the factors which enabled some Americans to move into the ranks of the independent proprietors while others remained bookkeepers, clerks, or salesmen, we shall better understand what is too often vaguely referred to as the middle classes.[28]

It is more difficult to make even preliminary judgments about the mobility of men in the industrial labor force. For a long time there was a great gap between the skilled and the unskilled. It is likely that those among the latter who sought to move upward found fewer opportunities in step-by-step promotion within the plant than in somehow breaking away from it to strike out on their own as contractors or businessmen or as politicians or labor organizers. More recently the development of industrial unions, along with closed shop and seniority practices, may have altered that situation, but to what extent remains to be measured.[29]

Some of these phenomena become more comprehensible in the light of the historic changes in the structure of the American family. In other societies, the character of the household, marriage patterns, and the relations of parents to children vitally affected the transmission of property, the definition of goals, and the degree of social mobility. None of these connections has been explored for the United States. The facile generalizations about the family as "a property institution dominated by middle class standards" are almost meaningless. And such schematic interpretations as usually describe the evolution of the "nuclear family" reveal little about the actual phasing and import of the changes in it. One could not now say with assurance, for instance, when marriage became the product of an autonomous decision of the partners, among which social groups, or in what regions. Yet this was certainly a crucial element in determining the rate of social mobility.[30]

One approach toward understanding these problems is through an examination of the ethnic elements in social mobility. The heterogeneous groups that constituted American society were drawn from dissimilar cultural backgrounds and displayed dissimilar attitudes toward the employment of capital, the value of savings, the use of windfalls, the assumption of risks, and the objectives of life. They exhibited also different patterns of consumption, of social control, and of kinship behavior. Such factors created variant patterns of expectation that shaped the motivation and the capacity for performance of the individuals who grew up within them. In addition, the members of these groups possessed connections and enjoyed prestige or suffered from discrimination to varying degrees. There were significant differences in their ability to locate themselves in desirable occupations.

Internal migration often juxtaposed in a single community groups derived from diverse backgrounds, each marked with its own cultural traits. Differences in the rate of social mobility among them may offer significant clues to the determinants of the pace of movement. Cities just behind the frontier line — Pittsburgh or Cincinnati in the 1830's, San Francisco or St. Louis in the 1850's, Cleveland in the 1880's — were distinguished by peculiar combinations of restraint and opportunity. There Yankees and Southerners, Irishmen and Germans, each in the particularity of his own heritage, competed for the prizes of advancement. Who gained, and how much, was a measure of the qualities that counted.[31]

The rewards were genuine and within reach of many who strove for them. This was the tenor of the vast literature of success evoked by the experience of the American economy. Each period gave the theme its own variations. Cotton Mather extolled Sir William Phips who earned gold and godliness too; Ben Franklin praised the shrewdly calculating tradesman; Horatio Alger traced the rise from rags to riches through pluck and luck; and Frank Norris described the elemental struggle of the fittest to survive. How far the myth conformed to reality we shall know better when we understand the relation of the political, social, and educational systems to the diffusion of property. But, whatever the reality, the myth expressed a deeply held faith that the power to seek wealth was open to all and furthered the liberty of all.[32]

The consistent failure of occasional efforts to restrict the movement of individuals from one social level to another confirmed the belief that the rewards of the economic order were available to all Americans. The operations of potent forces kept American society fluid and frustrated all such attempts.

Although the number of *rentiers* in the United States was probably larger than has commonly been supposed, they never acquired the coherence of an organized group and were rarely able to transmit their incomes intact from one generation to another. The law did not favor institutional devices that tended in that direction; and the dominant factors in an expanding economy, generally prone to inflation, were hostile.

Nor did an aristocratic landed gentry develop in the American colonies despite the English background and despite the experience of colonial settlement elsewhere. The fragile beginnings of such a group in the plantation South and along the Hudson and Connecticut rivers in the North had no capacity for sustained growth. The putative American gentry proved incapable of maintaining their situation for more than one or two generations. The factors which rendered them unstable and deprived them of control cannot be ascribed simply to the Revolution. More complex elements were involved — the nature of the labor force that discouraged all large-scale agricultural enterprise, the difficulty of institutionalizing landed property, and the absence of a stable community, at the apex of which the squire could locate himself.[33]

A far more complex effort to acquire elite status absorbed the energies of the various occupational groups which struggled for recognition as professions. By the opening of the eighteenth century there was a widening distinction between the conditions of lawyers, physicians, ministers, and professors in America and their counterparts in England. In 1699, for example, the Attorney-General of New York was a man "bred to a trade and neither to learning nor to the law." As the number of practitioners grew in the New World, there were occasional attempts to emulate the mother country by restricting the admission of newcomers. Nevertheless, access to these callings remained relatively free, a condition no doubt connected with their loss of unique status in the community which exposed them to the general American hostility to restrictive privilege.[34]

The struggle for the definition of professional status continued through the nineteenth century in a variety of spheres. An adjustment was not ultimately arrived at until early in the twentieth century, and only at the expense of a radical modification of the very conception of what a profession was. The license was then restored as a selective device; it was, however, no longer a grant of privilege, but rather a mode of police regulation that extended to a multitude of skills, to those of barbers and electricians as well as physicians and lawyers.

Through this long history the heirs of traditional professions, like law and medicine, faced complex problems. They had to beat off the competition from such purveyors of rival services as midwives, apothecaries, and accountants. They had to demonstrate the greater effectiveness of their own skills over the self-help of patent medicines and legal handbooks. At the same time, the steady increase in population led to a rising demand for professional aid.

These circumstances dictated the strategy of the struggle for position. Any increase in the numbers of doctors or lawyers diluted the privileges of the entrenched practitioners. Two alternatives were open to those who wished to preserve or add to those privileges — either to limit the new entries by excluding outsiders or to define, and achieve recognition for, stratified categories of practice that would protect a select inner group while opening the general field to competition. In either case, the result was a subtle change in the very conception of what the profession was.

There were few institutional means of attaining these goals. The authority of tradition was not binding; and the members of occupational groups that sought elite status displayed a significantly ambiguous attitude toward the state. They desired the support of government in excluding outsiders, yet resisted as an intrusion any suggestion of government regulation. Instead, they insisted that codes of ethics which they could promulgate themselves would be adequate to take care of any public interest that might be involved. Hence the importance, in their view, of a prescribed course of education which not only transmitted skills but also selected eligible novices and developed in them an *esprit de corps*. In effect, the practitioners sought to become a self-contained and self-perpetuating body of men with effective control over an important avenue of upward social mobility.

No profession wholly succeeded in making such a place for itself, although medicine came closest to doing so. That calling offers a very useful field for the examination of these forces, both because of the high position it acquired and because of its relation to government and education. From the Revolution to the last two decades of the nineteenth century there was a steady loosening of professional controls. There was, correspondingly, ever greater freedom to take up the art of healing, although proper antecedents and social position were still important in achieving eminence. From 1880 to 1940 the tendency toward relative ease of entry was reversed. Legal and educational regulations grew tighter and admission to the ranks of the physicians grew steadily more restrictive. After 1940, some of the exclusionary tendencies all but disappeared, without, however, a relaxation of professional standards. Medical, like engineering schools, could no longer discriminate against applicants on the basis of religious or ethnic antecedents in the face of the acute shortage of qualified practitioners and of the social disapproval of such manifestations of bias.

A careful study of the various phases of this development in terms broad enough to take in all the elements that influenced the recruitment of doctors and the status of the medical profession would show the importance of the influence the physicians commanded through their connections with the university, the government, and powerful social groups, and through the unique aura of their role as healers.[35] No other profession was able to establish the same degree of control, although some attained partial, qualified success. The lawyers were never able to achieve a limitation in the total number of practitioners; but they evolved a significant equivalent through internal stratification. Teachers, although generally conceded professional status and esteem, exercised only slight control over entry to their calling. By way of contrast, the notary or conveyancer who had a position of genuine importance in Europe lost it completely in the United States. Finally, a large number of callings which have sought recognition have as yet only partially been conceded it — morticians, realtors, accountants, and businessmen.[36]

The process of defining the professions was animated by a sustained effort to restrict freedom of access to a strategic group of occupations and to limit social mobility. Whatever success that effort had was conditioned by the necessity for transforming the concept of a profession into a form justifiable by the criteria of the whole society, that is, into a medium for maintaining standards to protect the public. The result was always to leave some liberty for movement into the occupation.

The most striking attempt to create a truly oligarchic restrictive elite met with complete failure. Between 1880 and 1930 an inchoate and ill-defined but nevertheless significant movement sought to establish a grouping, based upon birth as well as upon wealth, that would somehow exercise the kind of social and political leadership ascribed to European aristocracy. Historians who have paid any attention to it at all, have been disposed to treat the effort to define "society" as the eccentric whim of eccentric ladies eager for prestige. Yet the movement had a significant, even though unrealized, potential. It arose in response to shifts in the locus of wealth and power in the wake of massive industrialization. It was related to the control of great fortunes; it developed an ideology and a program; it exerted a profound influence upon American society, law, and culture; it briefly entered politics; and it posed subtle questions about the premises of American democracy and freedom.[37]

The effort failed. The political institutions proved resistant; the social underpinnings were shaky; and wealth could not be channeled into the hands only of those who thought it their due. Above all, those who aspired to be aristocrats misunderstood the role of leadership in a free society. The elite in the United States was not monolithic, but fragmented. Since the population was heterogeneous and was occupied in a variety of uncoordinated activities and associations, no single line of assent organized the whole people as a following. Leaders secured the support of particular segments with which they had institutional relations, but even they could count on their followings only within the terms of those limited relations. Respect and loyalty earned in politics, religion, or business did not of itself carry over into other spheres.[38]

The paths toward status and riches remained open — not to the same width for all men at all times, but enough to keep alive the faith that the goods of society were widely available. Power directed toward the goal of increasing wealth received the consent of the people because it promised to expand their liberty.

The persistance of social mobility had weighty consequences for the nation as well as for its citizens. It may be hypothesized that talent, free to express itself, moved where it was needed and leveled the barriers that impeded economic development in traditional or caste-bound societies. The stimulus to self-realization and autonomy destroyed the restraints of habit and inertia and encouraged spontaneity and originality. Despite the heavy personal strains that mobility sometimes entailed, these were among the most precious rewards of freedom.[39]

☆ VIII ☆

QUESTIONS
OF CHRONOLOGY
AND CAUSE

THE tone of pessimism that has run through much of the speculation about the future of liberty deserves understanding. It was not the product of any particular crisis, grave as many have been. Nor was it the reaction simply of frightened men of little faith.

Some of the most thoughtful students of American society have expressed doubts about the capacity of the free institutions of the United States to survive. "Only a remarkable, accidental and inherently temporary set of conditions made it possible, for a time, for such a 'free' social system — private initiative in economic life and government through representative institutions — to seem to work," concluded an acute scholar in 1947. "The whole view of politics as the adjustment of individual private claims" was dying, wrote a British observer in 1944, for "the old individualism which was the philosophical basis of American jurisprudence" was already dead.[1]

Such somber predictions and warnings have been as characteristic of the past as of the present. More than a century ago, De Tocqueville perceived the signs of a "species of oppression" in the United States "unlike anything that ever before existed in the world," one which compressed and stupified people until they were "reduced to nothing better than a flock of timid and industrious animals, of which the government" was the shepherd. Such a government not only oppressed men but stripped them of all human qualities.[2] These trepidations were scarcely less frequently expressed than the confidence in an ever-ascending procession toward freedom.

The time has not yet come to cast up the account, to arrive at a judgment on whether freedom has waxed or waned. But it seems hardly likely that the grim forebodings of men at any given point in the past were the products of deliberate calculations of the whole course of development even in their own times. More probably these conclusions were responses to the threat to particular aspects of the liberty they valued.

All too often the strategy of debate has led Americans to identify liberty with one or another of the negative safeguards that were but its external props. The entering wedge, the breach in the dike, the road with no turning — these recurrent figures of speech have summoned them to battle in defense of some principle upon which the whole fate of freedom seemed to hinge.

However worthy were these causes, those who fought for them were in error. Liberty did not depend upon any single feature of American society; it was bound in with the total development of the nation. It was no simple phenomenon resting upon one keystone or comprehensible from a particular point of view. It was the way of life of a people who wished so to order their institutions that they would be able themselves to make the decisions important to them.

The earlier chapters of this volume have defined the several themes in terms of which the history of American liberty can be described. That was necessary to make clear the dimensions of a larger task. But that effort was not intended to obscure what was most important of all — the interrelations among those themes. The views afforded by the various perspectives from which liberty was regarded revealed that it constituted, after all, but a single subject — the way in which men pursued their hopes for achievement by cooperating voluntarily or by consenting to be governed.

The free American was an individual who wished to expand his capacity for action by increasing the number of choices available to him. He sought the company of others, but under terms that would release not bind him. He used rather than feared coercive power because he could control it by protective procedures which transformed violence into mutual consent.

The free man accepted these terms of his freedom because experience demonstrated its advantages. The gains of common effort, diffused through the society, gave all a stake in it. The free man also developed the means of acting without constraint. The experience of migration and the problems of living among strangers taught him the modes of voluntary association which added to his power without binding him. Finally, he worked out the means of applying restraint at the points at which it was necessary through procedures to which he himself consented.

To describe these complex developments adequately calls for a treatment which will reveal the interplay among them. That can only come within a chronological context.

The story falls into five major periods.

For some three-quarters of the seventeenth century the American experiment remained tentative. Along the coast scattered settlements of Europeans attempted to reconstruct the whole communities they had left at home. They failed as other immigrants who followed them also would. But the settlements took root because the New World held promises of its own to compensate for its frustrations. Although the first planters still subscribed to the rigid conceptions of status they brought with them, they made their way toward the attainment of their own ends, which they learned to disassociate from those of the community. And they sketched the outlines of new political and social orders, differing substantially among themselves, yet all bearing the distinct impress of patterns derived from across the ocean and all modified by experience in the wilderness.

Between the closing decades of the seventeenth century and the American Revolution, the new society took form. The final assertion of British sovereignty over all the colonies and a common situation that transcended the particular differences of condition between Maine and Georgia created a mode of life that bound these people together. Rapid expansion and local autonomy were the dominant conditions; individualism, fragmented communities with a plurality of social organizations, and government by citizens jealous of their rights were the results. Independence was but the formal recognition of a change that had already occurred. The Americans emerged from the war with a state which they hoped would serve the common good as effectively as those of Europe served their rulers.

For almost a century thereafter Americans tested the consequences of having become a republic. The imperatives of action in a Commonwealth proved different from those which operated in the old regimes. The obligation to subject all measures to the test of the common good and the suspicion of privilege in an order which men had created rather than inherited required a dispersal of power and led to the development of a loosely articulated mechanism of government. Meanwhile, continued expansion put unprecedented riches at the disposal of the society and gave it a fluidity that enabled it to meet successive crises at home and abroad.

The new governments created during the War for Independence proved capable of adjusting to the changing demands upon them. An impressive array of other organizations took form effectively to serve the needs of a highly mobile population. The commonwealth idea faded away to be replaced by faith in the competence of individuals to seek their own welfare to the ultimate advantage of them all. Sustained by an overriding confidence in the goodness of man and his ability to mold nature according to his will, that faith seemed capable of solving all problems. Only Negro slavery remained a glaring exception, and that ultimately led to the tragic trial of war.

Between 1870 and 1940 the institutions that had survived the Civil War passed through a complex development. The wounds of battle healed and the economy grew at an unprecedented rate. The promise of abundant rewards for all seemed about to be redeemed.

Yet, beneath the scars of apparent recovery from the war, old sores festered and the rapid social changes of industrialization created new problems along with the wealth. The competition that stimulated expansion left many individuals unprovided for; and the fragmented communities within which Americans organized themselves struggled feverishly to keep apace of the mounting demands upon them.

Already by the turn of the century, some men called for greater order, for the use of intelligence and control to deal with the imposing problems of the times. At first they sought to operate through existing voluntary media; after 1900 their hopes more often turned upon a broadening of the regulatory, policing, functions of the state. The First World War radically expanded the scope of government action. That trend was temporary but it created precedents for the renewal and further broadening of governmental activities during the depression of the 1930's. By then the underlying view of what the state could do had significantly changed. Increasingly some Americans turned to it in the hope that it could plan orderly economic and social development. The great inner conflicts of the last decade of the period revolved about the pace and extent of the change in the light of the concomitant transformations of the way power was organized and administered.

Twenty years of war and cold war since 1940 have done little to dissolve earlier uncertainties. The tendencies of the 1930's were not reversed, despite the alternation in office of groups with divergent political philosophies. To some extent the new configuration of relations between the state, the power apparatus, and the individual was a product of the challenge of external threats to the security of the nation. It also derived from, or was connected to, the altered situation and values of a metropolitan culture transformed by technology and desperately eager for security and stability. Only against the total record of the past will it be possible to measure the consequences for liberty of these most recent changes.

The troubling questions of causes and consequences we postpone for the moment. All too many grandiose, inclusive explanations have linked the development of liberty to a single cause. It will not do to say that any one of them is wholly right or wholly wrong. But none, in its present formulation, seems altogether adequate.

A long line of political speculation has associated free institutions with the widespread diffusion of private property. The conviction of Aristotle that the most desirable political community rested on a "middle class" base extended down to the philosphers of the Enlightenment on both sides of the Atlantic. In the American context that proposition was often capped by the corollary that liberty emanated from the frontier which made land universally available to a society of yeoman farmers. Aristotle's assumption could also be applied to the United States in terms of the effects of industrialism, urbanization, and capitalism.[3]

Another trend of interpretation has accounted for the

development of liberty by reference to spiritual impulses associated with the Judeo-Christian heritage, or more specifically with Protestantism, or more specifically still with Puritanism. The fatherhood of God and the brotherhood of man nurtured the seeds of faith in the dignity of the human personality of which free institutions were the worldly expressions.[4]

Finally, it has been possible to regard liberty as the product of national character. The numerous variants upon this theme range from the racist writers who supposed that freedom had been born in the German forests and was transmitted in the blood stream of the Teutonic folk, to the scholars who sought its origins in Anglo-Saxon law, to the modern students who have traced the will to be free to family structure, patterns of child-rearing, and personality traits.[5]

It would be consoling to predict that some more comprehensive synthesis will draw elements of all these interpretations together. We make, however, no pretense to optimism about our ability to arrive at such a synthesis. We aim now primarily to keep the potentialities of such explanations in mind as we deal with the concrete problems of the American past.

Nor shall we venture yet to outline the specific social consequences of liberty. Believing as we do that it was bound in with every aspect of the American way of life, we assume that it had a pronounced effect upon the productive system, the forms of government, and the character of the people. Our task will be to trace that effect by exploring the demonstrable connections between freedom and the American institutions it influenced.

The current awareness of the importance of doing so is encouraging. The scholars in many fields are conscious of the obligation to look beyond the limits of their own discipline in the search for causes. Few, for instance, would reject in principle the proposition that the really fundamental problems of economic growth are noneconomic and consist of "generating and energizing human action."[6] Yet in practice it is often tempting to treat the "stages" of economic growth as if they existed altogether apart from their social and cultural context, to suppose that industrialism can be applied in much the same way to any community just as earlier Americans believed that representative government could.[7]

The questions that need answers are of a more specific order. Have loose political controls influenced the process of capital formation, the receptivity to innovation, the ability to absorb the costs of mistakes, and the modes of disbursing the products of industry? Was the altered meaning of political consent in the second quarter of the nineteenth century connected with changes in the patterns and rates of social mobility? Was the intensification of voluntary activities in the last quarter of that century a result of distrust of the political process, or was it a product of other forces that merely diverted energies away from politics? The task involved in assembling the data that will permit a confrontation of such problems has been outlined in this book.

It deserves the best efforts that can be given it. For it may well be that our time will best be remembered for its painful and tenuous, yet immensely exhilarating, effort to allow men to be free.

NOTES
ACKNOWLEDGMENTS
INDEX

NOTES

INTRODUCTION

1. Isaiah Berlin, *Two Concepts of Liberty* (Oxford, 1958), 57.
2. For a nonhistorical study of these ideas, see Mortimer J. Adler, *The Idea of Freedom* (Garden City, 1958), xix, 98, *passim*.

CHAPTER I. LIBERTY AND POWER

1. Thomas Hobbes, *Leviathan or the Matter, Forme and Power of a Commonwealth*, ed. Michael Oakeshott (Oxford, 1957), 84, 136, 137; Isaiah Berlin, *Two Concepts of Liberty* (Oxford, 1958), 12.
2. Mortimer J. Adler, *The Idea of Freedom* (Garden City, 1958), 112ff.; H. M. Kallen, *Freedom in the Modern World* (New York, 1928), 272.
3. Adler, *Idea of Freedom*, 134ff.; Alfred North Whitehead, *Adventures of Ideas* (New York [1933]), 84.
4. The philosophical issue is stated in Adler, *Idea of Freedom*, 87ff.; also Marshall Cohen, "Berlin and the Liberal Tradition," *Philosophical Quarterly*, x (1960), 216ff.
5. Among the best of such works are: Zechariah Chafee, Jr., *Free Speech in the United States* (Cambridge, Mass., 1941); Zechariah Chafee, Jr., *Government and Mass Communications* (Chicago, 1947), I; Anson Phelps Stokes, *Church and State in the United States* (New York, 1950); Gustavus Myers, *History of Bigotry in the United States* (New York, 1943); Richard Hofstadter and Walter P. Metzger, *The Development of Academic Freedom in the United States* (New York, 1955).
6. Oswald Garrison Villard, *The Disappearing Daily* (New York, 1944), 19ff.
7. Loren P. Beth, *American Theory of Church and State* (Gainesville, 1958), 33ff. See also above, 73.

8. Whitehead, *Adventures of Ideas*, 78.

9. Whitehead, *Adventures of Ideas*, 74; Karl Mannheim, *Ideology and Utopia* (New York [1936]), 107.

10. See Norval Morris, *The Habitual Criminal* (Cambridge, Mass., 1951), 357 ff.; Aito Ahto, *Dangerous Habitual Criminals* (Helsinki, 1951), 130ff.; Glenn Whitney, "Freedom is Frightful," *Boston Sunday Globe*, June 5, 1960, p. 54; Erich Fromm, *Escape from Freedom* (New York [1941]).

11. There are suggestive insights in Elie A. Cohen, *Human Behavior in the Concentration Camp*, trans. M. H. Braaksma (New York [1953]), 125ff., 173ff.; David Rousset, *The Other Kingdom*, trans. Ramon Guthrie (New York [1947]), 100ff., 167; Stanley M. Elkins, *Slavery a Problem in American Institutional and Intellectual Life* (Chicago [1959]), 103ff.

12. See Aldous Huxley, *Brave New World* (London, 1958), xiii; George Orwell, *Nineteen Eighty-Four* (London, 1949), 18, 55, 71ff.

13. Whitehead, *Adventures of Ideas*, 86; Adler, *Idea of Freedom*, 602–603.

14. A. J. Ayer, *Philosophical Essays* (London, 1954), 278–281; A. E. Ellis, *The Rack* (London [1958]).

15. David Hume, *An Enquiry Concerning the Human Understanding*, ed. L. A. Selby-Bigge (Oxford, 1894), 95; Jonathan Edwards, *Freedom of the Will*, ed. Paul Ramsey (New Haven, 1957), 163.

16. Hobbes, *Leviathan*, 137.

17. John Dewey, *Experience and Education* (New York, 1950), 74.

18. For other illustrations, see Voltaire, *Dictionaire philosophique* (Paris, 1816), x, 232; John Locke, *Essay Concerning Human Understanding*, ed. A. C. Fraser (Oxford, 1894), I, 324–331, 366ff.; John Stuart Mill, *On Liberty and Considerations on Representative Government*, ed. R. B. McCallum (Oxford, 1946), 1, 11; Frank H. Knight, "The Meaning of Freedom," Charner M. Perry, ed., *The Philosophy of American Democracy* (Chicago [1943]), 68, 78ff.

19. Adler, *Idea of Freedom*, 100, 601ff.

20. Hobbes, *Leviathan*, 56ff.

21. These observations are compatible with a variety of psychological and anthropological interpretations. See: Lord Raglan, *The Hero* (New York, 1937), 268ff.; M. Fortes and E. E. Evans-Pritchard, *African Political Systems* (London, 1958), 16ff.; E. Adamson Hoebel, *The Law of Primitive Man* (Cambridge, Mass., 1954), 257ff.; Sigmund Freud, *Totem and Taboo*, trans. A. Brill (London [1930]), 26off.

22. "A Coppie of the Liberties of the Massachusets Collonie in New England" (1641), Massachusetts Historical Society, *Collections, Third Series* (Boston, 1843), VIII, 234.

23. Samuel M. Bemiss, *The Three Charters of the Virginia Company of London* (Williamsburg, 1957), 9. See also above, 26ff.

CHAPTER II. THE PROCEDURES FOR THE
EXERCISE OF POWER

1. Evarts B. Greene, *The Provincial Governor in the English Colonies of North America* (Cambridge, [1898]), 23; Henry Wharton, *Life of John Smith English Soldier,* trans. Laura P. Striker (Chapel Hill [1957]), 75.

2. "Complaint of the Eight Men to the Amsterdam Chamber, 1644," E. B. O'Callaghan and Berthold Fernow, eds., *Documents Relative to the Colonial History of the State of New York* (Albany, 1856–87), I, 213; Roger Vailland, *The Law,* trans. Peter Wiles (New York, 1958), 43.

3. John Locke, *Two Treatises of Government,* ed. Thomas I. Cook (New York, 1947), Second Treatise, secs. 22, 57, pp. 132, 148.

4. Leonidas Dodson, *Alexander Spotswood Governor of Colonial Virginia* (Philadelphia, 1932), 30; Arthur M. Schlesinger, *Prelude to Independence* (New York, 1958), 25; See also Edmund S. Morgan, *John Winthrop and the Puritan Dilemma* (Boston, 1958), 155ff.; Leonard W. Labaree, *Royal Government in America* (New Haven, 1930), 35, 179ff., 312ff.; Greene, *Provincial Governor,* 166ff.; Wilcomb E. Washburn, *The Governor and the Rebel* (Chapel Hill [1957]), 157ff.; Louis K. Koontz, *Robert Dinwiddie* (Glendale, 1941), 201ff.

5. T. J. Haarhoff, *The Stranger at the Gate* (Oxford, 1948); Charlotte B. Goodfellow, *Roman Citizenship* ([Lancaster], 1935), 7ff., 41ff.; A. N. Sherwin-White, *Roman Citizenship* (Oxford, 1939); Locke, *Two Treatises,* Second Treatise, sec. 118, p. 181; Robert F. Seybolt, *Colonial Citizen of New York* (Madison, 1918); Carl Brinkmann, *Recent Theories of Citizenship* (New Haven, 1927), 13ff.

6. The paraphrase is from John Stuart Mill, *On Liberty and Considerations on Representative Government,* ed. R. B. McCallum (Oxford, 1946), 101. For the discrepancy between English and colonial conceptions of the alien, see "Report of the Council of New-York and Mr. Livingston's Memorial, 1696," O'Callaghan and Fernow, *Documents Relative to the Colonial History of New York,* IV, 204–253. For the equality of native and naturalized citizens see Chief Justice Marshall in *Osborn* v. *Bank of the United States,* 9 Wheaton 738, 827 (1824); also John P. Roche, *Early Development of United States Citizenship* (Ithaca, 1949), 7ff.

7. Charles P. Daly, *Naturalization Embracing the Past History of the Subject, and the Present State of the Law* (New York, 1860); Joseph Willard, *Naturalization in the American Colonies with More Particular Reference to Massachusetts* (Boston, 1859); Frank G. Franklin, *Legislative History of Naturalization in the United States from the Revolutionary War to 1861* (Chicago, 1906); Westel W.

Willoughby, *Constitutional Law of the United States* (New York, 1929), I, 379ff.; Luella Gettys, *Law of Citizenship in the United States* (Chicago [1934]), 21ff.; Frederick Van Dyne, *Citizenship of the United States* (Rochester, 1904), 54ff.

8. *Magna Carta*, Article 42, ed. J. C. Dickinson (London, 1955), 24; "A Coppie of the Liberties of the Massachusets Collonie in New England," Massachusetts Historical Society, *Collections, Third Series* (Boston, 1843), VIII, 219; [Gaillard Hunt], *The American Passport, Its History* (Washington, 1898); Van Dyne, *Citizenship*, 251ff.; Association of the Bar of the City of New York, *Freedom to Travel. Report of the Special Committee to Study Passport Procedures* (New York, 1958).

9. 15 *Statutes at Large*, 223; *Opinions of the Principal Officers of the Executive Departments and Other Papers Relating to Expatriation, Naturalization and Change of Allegiance* (Washington, 1873), 10, 98; John Randolph, *Substance of a Speech Delivered in a Committee of the Whole House of Representatives on Thursday the 6th of March, 1806* (n.p., n.d.); [Tench Coxe], *Examination of the Conduct of Great Britain* (Philadelphia, 1807), 33ff.; I-Mien Tsiang, *The Question of Expatriation in America Prior to 1907* (Baltimore, 1942), 25ff.; Frederick Van Dyne, *A Treatise on the Law of Naturalization of the United States* (Washington, 1907), 333ff.; Van Dyne, *Citizenship*, 269ff. A contrary, but unrepresentative, view is presented in [John Lowell], *Review of a Treatise on Expatriation by George Hay, Esquire* (Boston, 1814). See also Gettys, *Law of Citizenship*, 160ff.

10. John P. Roche, "Pre-Statutory Denaturalization," *Cornell Law Quarterly*, XXXV (1949), 120ff.; and "The Loss of American Nationality — the Development of Statutory Expatriation," *University of Pennsylvania Law Review*, XCIX (1950), 25ff.; and "Loss of American Nationality: the Years of Confusion," *Western Political Quarterly*, IV (1951), 268ff.; and "Statutory Denaturalization," *Pittsburgh Law Review*, XIII (1952), 276ff.

11. See Cortlandt F. Bishop, *History of Elections in the American Colonies* (New York, 1893), 69ff.; also Daniel Webster, "First Settlement of New England" (1820), *Works* (4th ed., Boston, 1853), I, 36, 39; John T. Horton, *James Kent: a Study in Conservatism* (New York, 1939), 255.

12. Albert J. McCulloch, *Suffrage and Its Problems* (Baltimore, 1929), 99, 166ff.; Kirk A. Porter, *History of Suffrage in the United States* (Chicago [1918]), 116ff.

13. See Locke, *Two Treatises*, (First Treatise, sec. 101, Second Treatise, secs. 2, 52–67, 85), 74, 121, 146ff., 162; Oscar Handlin, *Race and Nationality in American Life* (Boston, 1957), 15ff.; Eleanor Flexner, *Century of Struggle. The Woman's Rights Movement in the United States* (Cambridge, Mass., 1959), 7ff.; Zechariah Chafee, Jr.,

Free Speech in the United States (Cambridge, Mass., 1941), 196ff., 439ff.

14. Jerome R. Reich, *Leisler's Rebellion* (Chicago [1953]), 112ff.; Oscar and Mary Handlin, *Commonwealth, A Study of the Role of Government in the American Economy* (New York, 1947), 15.

15. Handlin, *Commonwealth*, 5ff.

16. Locke, *Two Treatises*, 168ff.

17. Thomas Paine, *American Crisis* (London, 1819), 10.

18. James Morton Smith, ed., *Seventeenth-Century America. Essays in Colonial History* (Chapel Hill [1959]), 4ff.

19. See, e.g., Samuel W. McCall, *The Liberty of Citizenship* (New Haven, 1915), 116ff.; also Arthur W. Macmahon, ed., *Federalism, Mature and Emergent* (Garden City, 1955); also, above, 51ff.

20. *Federalist Papers*, no. 47, ed. E. G. Bourne (New York, 1901), I, 329ff.; Ellen E. Brennan, *Plural Office-Holding in Massachusetts* (Chapel Hill, 1945); Jerome Frank, *If Men Were Angels* (New York [1942]), 236ff.

21. See, e.g., Charles Warren, *The Supreme Court in United States History* (rev. ed., Boston, 1937); Greene, *Provincial Governor;* Edward S. Corwin, *The President Office and Powers* (2d ed., New York [1941]); W. E. Binkley, *President and Congress* (Garden City, 1947).

22. *Federalist Papers*, no. 39, I, 257; Alexander Hamilton, "Brief of Argument on the Constitution" (1788), *Works*, ed. H. C. Lodge (New York, 1904), II, 91ff.

23. Koenraad W. Swart, *Sale of Office in the Seventeenth Century* ('s-Gravenhage, 1949); Franklin L. Ford, *Robe and Sword* (Cambridge, Mass., 1953); Hans Rosenberg, *Bureaucracy, Aristocracy and Autocracy* (Cambridge, Mass., 1958).

24. See "Fundamental Agreement, or Original Constitution of the Colony of New-Haven, June 4, 1639," Francis N. Thorpe, *Federal and State Constitutions* (Washington, 1909), I, 525. For the distinction between livery and yeomanry in the government of companies here referred to, see George Unwin, *The Gilds and Companies of London* (2d ed., London [1925]), 217. See also Connecticutensis, *Three Letters to Abraham Bishop* (Hartford, 1800), 13.

25. S. G. Nissenson, *Patroon's Domain* (New York, 1937).

26. Amitai Etzioni, "Alternative Ways to Democracy," *Political Science Quarterly*, LXXIV (1959), 212ff.

27. Frederick W. Dallinger, *Nominations for Elective Office in the United States* (New York, 1903), 4ff.; Bishop, *Elections in the Colonies*, 120ff.

28. *Federalist Papers*, no. 10, I, 62ff. See also Neal Riemer, "James Madison's Theory of the Self-Destructive Features of Republican Government," *Ethics*, LXV (1954), 34ff.

29. See *Niles' Weekly Register*, September 13, 20, 1823; W. E.

Binkley, *American Political Parties* (New York, 1943); V. O. Key, Jr., *Politics, Parties, and Pressure Groups* (New York, 1958); Dixon Ryan Fox, *Decline of Aristocracy in the Politics of New York* (New York, 1919), 271ff., 352ff. The only serious questioning of the principle of consent through representation came in the exclusion of legislators from the bodies to which they were elected, because of their political or religious views. See Chafee, *Free Speech in the United States*, 252ff., 269ff.

30. See the definitions in *A New English Dictionary on Historical Principles* (Oxford, 1888–), VIII, 1069.

31. [William Tudor], "Report of the Committee Appointed by the General Assembly of the State of Rhode-Island," *Monthly Anthology*, VII (1809), 194; T. H. Reed, *Municipal Government in the United States* (New York, 1926), 34ff.; Society for the Reformation of Juvenile Delinquents in the City of New-York, *First Annual Report of the Managers* (New York, 1825); August Vollmer and Alfred E. Parker, *Crime and the State Police* (Berkeley, 1935), 14ff.; J. A. Fairlie, *Local Government in Counties, Towns, and Villages* (New York, 1906), 109, 402; A. E. Costello, *Our Police Protectors History of the New York Police* (New York, 1885), 12; E. H. Savage, *Chronological History of the Boston Watch and Police* (Boston, 1865), 12, 20, 25ff., 60, 67.

32. Raymond B. Fosdick, *American Police Systems* (New York, 1920), 67ff.; Z. S. Eldredge, *Beginnings of San Francisco, 1912*), II, 603ff.; "Report on New York Police," New York City Common Council, *Document No. 54* (1844); Savage, *Chronological History of the Boston Watch*, 100ff.

33. Vollmer and Parker, *Crime and the State Police*, 75ff., 145. In some places there were antecedents in state constables or inspectors.

34. Max Lowenthal, *The Federal Bureau of Investigation* (New York, 1950), 3ff.

35. Henry C. Corbin and Frederick T. Wilson, *Federal Aid in Domestic Disturbances 1787–1903* (Washington, 1903), 55ff.

36. See *Federalist Papers*, nos. 78, 79, II, 98ff.; Albert J. Beveridge, *Life of John Marshall* (Boston [1919]), III, 50ff.; Brooks Adams, *The Theory of Social Revolutions* (New York, 1913), 36, 37, 68, 127.

37. Evan Haynes, *The Selection and Tenure of Judges* (National Conference of Judicial Councils, 1944), 17ff., 90ff.; Simeon Baldwin, *The American Judiciary* (New York, 1905), 50ff., 331ff.; Adams, *Theory of Social Revolutions*, 129, 225ff.; H. F. Stone, "The Issues Involved in the Methods of Selecting and Removing Judges," Academy of Political Science, *Proceedings*, III (1913), 124ff.; Learned Hand, "The Elective and Appointive Methods of Selection of Judges," *ibid.*, 130ff.; Gilbert E. Roe, "The Recall of Judges," *ibid.*, 141ff.; Charles A. Beard and Birl E. Schultz. *Documents on the State-Wide Initiative,*

Referendum and Recall (New York, 1912), 291ff.; Albert A. Stickney, *A True Republic* (New York, 1879), 204–205.

38. Roscoe Pound, *Organization of Courts* (Boston, 1940), 156; Baldwin, *American Judiciary*, 346, 382ff.; Jerome Frank, *Courts on Trial Myth and Reality in American Justice* (Princeton, 1949), 255ff.; James Bryce, *American Commonwealth* (New York, 1911), II, 683.

39. Paul P. Van Riper, *History of the United States Civil Service* (Evanston [1958]), 11ff.

40. Van Riper, *History of United States Civil Service*, 6off.; also Herman Finer, *The British Civil Service* (London, 1933).

41. Mill, *On Liberty*, 102; See also Walter Gellhorn, *Federal Administrative Proceedings* (Baltimore, 1941); Frank, *If Men Were Angels*, 190ff.; Homer Cummings, *Liberty Under Law and Administration* (New York, 1934), 110–114, 120, 121, 130ff. Charles S. Hyneman, *Bureaucracy in a Democracy* (New York [1950]), 38ff.; Van Riper, *History of United States Civil Service*, 533ff.

42. See William Kornhauser, *The Politics of Mass Society* (Glencoe [1959]), 227.

43. See Clarence H. Faust, "The Rhetoric of the Debate over the Adoption of the Constitutions," C. M. Perry, *Philosophy of American Democracy* (Chicago [1943]), 31ff.

44. The quotation is from Lincoln's first inaugural address, Abraham Lincoln, *Selected Writings and Speeches* (Chicago, 1943), 120; also *Federalist Papers*, no. 41, I, 278.

CHAPTER III. THE LIMITS OF POLITICAL POWER

1. See, in general, K. C. Wheare, *Federal Government* (Oxford, 1946); Arthur W. Macmahon, "The Problems of Federalism," Arthur W. Macmahon, ed., *Federalism, Mature and Emergent* (Garden City, 1955), 3ff.; Paul A. Freund, "Umpiring the Federal System," *ibid.*, 159ff.; also, above, 33.

2. Charles M. Andrews, *Colonial Period of American History* (New Haven, 1936), II, 1ff., 304ff.

3. Andrews, *Colonial Period*, II, 100ff.; Charles M. Andrews, *Beginnings of Connecticut* (New Haven, 1933), 51; also, above, 24.

4. Andrews, *Colonial Period*, II, 97–99; Charles M. Andrews, *Colonial Background of the American Revolution* (New Haven, 1924), 13; Viola F. Barnes, *Dominion of New England* (New Haven, 1923); Lawrence H. Gipson, *British Empire before the American Revolution* (New York, 1942), V, 113ff.

5. *Federalist Papers*, no. 20, ed. E. G. Bourne (New York, 1901), I, 134.

6. For an interesting analogy with the effects of practical conditions

in medieval England, see Roscoe Pound, Charles H. McIlwain, and Roy F. Nichols, *Federalism as a Democratic Process* (New Brunswick, 1942), 23, 39ff.

7. William Anderson, *The Nation and the States Rivals or Partners* (Minneapolis [1955]); Leonard D. White, *The States and the Nation* (Baton Rouge [1953]), 3ff.; Arthur N. Holcombe, "The Coercion of States in a Federal System," Macmahon, *Federalism*, 137ff.; Henry M. Hart, Jr., "The Relations between State and Federal Law," *ibid.*, 182ff.

8. Charles Warren, *The Supreme Court in United States History* (rev. ed., Boston, 1937), II, 206ff.; H. A. Millis, *Japanese Problem in the United States* (New York, 1915), 197ff.; Eliot G. Mears, *Resident Oriental on the American Pacific Coast* (Chicago [1928]), 157 ff.; Eugene V. Rostow, *National Policy for the Oil Industry* (New Haven, 1948), 21, 28ff.; J. Stanley Clark, *The Oil Century* (Norman [1958]), 189ff.; Jack Greenberg, *Race Relations and American Law* (New York, 1959), 243ff.; James J. Kilpatrick, *The Sovereign States* (Chicago, 1957); Henry Pelling, *American Labor* (Chicago [1960]), 205ff.

9. George C. S. Benson, *The New Centralization* (New York [1941]), 88ff., 116ff.; White, *States and the Nation*, 35ff.; Harold Zink, *Government of Cities in the United States* (New York, 1939), 37ff.; James E. Pate, *Local Government and Administration* (New York [1954]), 62ff.; Herbert Wechsler, "Political Safeguards of Federalism," Macmahon, *Federalism*, 97ff.; Anderson, *Nation and the States*, 214ff.

10. Andrews, *Colonial Background of the Revolution*, 194.

11. See, e.g., William Tudor, *The Life of James Otis of Massachusetts* (Boston, 1823), 69–70; Josiah Tucker, *Letter from a Merchant in London to His Nephew in North America* (London, 1766), 3–4; Andrews, *Colonial Background of the Revolution*, 199; also, above, 32.

12. Warren, *Supreme Court, passim* deals with many of these issues. Louis Hartz, *The Liberal Tradition in America* (New York [1955]), 9ff. stresses the Lockean basis.

13. The quotations are from Alexander Hamilton, "A Full Vindication" (1774), *Works*, ed. H. C. Lodge (New York, 1904), I, 6.

14. Benjamin F. Wright, *American Interpretations of Natural Law* (Cambridge, Mass., 1931), 149ff.

15. Russel B. Nye, *William Lloyd Garrison and the Humanitarian Reformers* (Boston [1955]), 141–143; J. Allen Smith, *The Spirit of American Government* (New York, 1907), 37–39; Charles A. Beard, *An Economic Interpretation of the Constitution of the United States* (New York, 1913), 324–325.

16. Hartz, *Liberal Tradition*, 281.

17. "A Coppie of the Liberties of the Massachusetts Collonie in New England," Massachusetts Historical Society, *Collections, Third Series* (Boston, 1843), VIII, 216ff.

18. Carl Becker, *The Declaration of Independence a Study in the History of Political Ideas* (New York, 1956), 24ff.; Robert A. Rutland, *The Birth of the Bill of Rights 1776–1791* (Chapel Hill [1955]), 31ff.; Richard L. Perry, *Sources of Our Liberties* ([Chicago] [1959]), 419ff.

19. Benjamin L. Oliver, *The Rights of an American Citizen* (Boston, 1832); Theophilus Parsons, *The Political, Personal, and Property Rights of a Citizen of the United States* (Hartford, 1874).

20. Oscar Handlin, *Race and Nationality in American Life* (Boston, 1957), 39ff.; Hartz, *Liberal Tradition*, 145ff.

21. Livingston Rutherford, *John Peter Zenger* (New York, 1941); Leonard W. Levy, *Legacy of Suppression Freedom of Speech and Press in Early American History* (Cambridge, Mass., 1960), 130ff.

22. Association of the Bar of the City of New York, *Freedom to Travel. Report of the Special Committee to Study Passport Procedures* (New York, 1958), 4, 5.

23. William O. Douglas, *The Right of the People* (New York, 1958), 87ff.; William Gellhorn, *American Rights: the Constitution in Action* (New York, 1960), 96ff.; Milton R. Konvitz, *Fundamental Liberties of a Free People* (Ithaca [1957]), 128ff.; Frederick F. Greenman, *Wire-Tapping. Its Relation to Civil Liberties* (Stamford, Conn. [1938]).

24. James Willard Hurst, *Law and the Conditions of Freedom in the Nineteenth-Century United States* (Madison, 1956), 3ff.

25. Richard Hofstadter and Walter P. Metzger, *The Development of Academic Freedom in the United States* (New York, 1955), 363ff.; Robert M. MacIver, *Academic Freedom in Our Time* (New York, 1955), 264ff.

26. There is a selection of legal materials in Sophonisba P. Breckinridge, *The Family and the State* (Chicago [1934]); see also Auguste Carlier, *Marriage in the United States*, trans. B. J. Jeffries (Boston, 1867), 34ff.; George E. Howard, *History of Matrimonial Institutions* (Chicago, 1904), II, 121ff., III, 161ff.; Perry, *Sources of Our Liberties*, 425ff.

27. *Federalist Papers*, no. 84, II, 152ff.; Rutland, *Birth of the Bill of Rights*, 132–133, 182; Charles Warren, *Making of the Constitution* (Cambridge, Mass., 1947), 506ff., 769ff.; Perry, *Sources of Our Liberties*, 403ff., 430; George Bancroft, *History of the Formation of the Constitution of the United States* (3d ed., New York, 1883), II, 247, 291ff.

28. John Locke, *Two Treatises of Government*, ed. Thomas I. Cook (New York, 1947), Second Treatise, sec. 6, p. 123; Thomas

Paine, "Rights of Man," *Political Writings* (Charleston, 1824), I, 73; John S. Mill, *On Liberty and Considerations of Representative Government*, ed. R. B. McCallum (Oxford, 1946), 66, 84, 79, 80, 97, 98.

29. Roscoe Pound, *The Development of Constitutional Guarantees of Liberty* (New Haven, 1957), 82ff.

30. The quotation is from Watson *v.* Jones (1872), 13 Wallace 679; see also Zechariah Chafee, Jr., *Free Speech in the United States* (Cambridge, Mass., 1941), 16, 32ff.; Levy, *Legacy of Suppression*, 249ff.

31. United States *v.* Miller (1939), 307 U.S. 174; Chafee, *Free Speech in the United States*, 73; Gellhorn, *American Rights*, 20ff.

32. On the patent system see Nathan Dane, *A General Abridgement and Digest of American Law* (Boston, 1823), I, 527; Joseph Barnes, *A Treatise on the Justice, Policy and Utility of Establishing an Effectual System for Promoting the Progress of Useful Arts by Assuming Property in the Products of Genius* (Philadelphia, 1792); E. Burke Inlow, *The Patent Grant* (Baltimore, 1950), 48ff., 69ff.; above p. 79. On freedom of contract see Roscoe Pound, "Liberty of Contract," *Yale Law Journal*, XVIII (1909), 454ff.; Arnold M. Paul, "Legal Progressivism, the Courts, and the Crisis of the 1890's," *Business History Review*, XXXIII (1959), 500. See also Benjamin R. Twiss, *Lawyers and the Constitution* (Princeton [1942]), 69ff.; Brooks Adams, *The Theory of Social Revolutions* (New York, 1913), 212, 213; Robert L. Hale, *Freedom Through Law* (New York, 1952), 385ff.; Loren P. Beth, *American Theory of Church and State* (Gainesville, 1958), 81–83.

33. Chafee, *Free Speech in the United States*, 27, 36ff.; Gellhorn, *American Rights*, 7ff., 41ff., 70ff.; Douglas, *Right of the People*, 17ff.

34. The popular attitude toward deportation expressed in Evangeline stands in striking contrast to the Indian removals a decade earlier. See Ernest Martin, *L' Evangéline de Longfellow* (Paris, 1936), 206ff.; also Warren, *Supreme Court in United States History*, I, 729ff.; Gellhorn, *American Rights*, 132ff.; Morton Grodzins, *Americans Betrayed* (Chicago [1949]), 351ff., 368ff.; Jacobus tenBroek, Edward N. Barnhart, and Floyd W. Matson, *Prejudice, War and the Constitution* (Berkeley, 1958), 211ff.

35. Douglas, *Right of the People*, 169ff.; Gellhorn, *American Rights*, 13.

36. Hartz, *Liberal Tradition*, 160ff. See also above, 128.

CHAPTER IV. THE ENDS OF THE USE OF POWER

1. The quotations are from the Mayflower Compact and the preamble to the federal constitution.

2. See Oscar and Mary F. Handlin, *Commonwealth, A Study of the Role of Government in the American Economy* (New York, 1947), 29ff.; James Harrington, *The Commonwealth of Oceana* (Henry Morley, ed., London, 1887),*passim*, and especially 19, 45; Caroline Robbins, *The Eighteenth-Century Commonwealthman* (Cambridge, 1959), 34ff.; George L. Haskins, *Law and Authority in Early Massachusetts* (New York, 1960), 59.

3. John Locke, *Two Treatises of Government*, ed. Thomas I. Cook (New York, 1947), Second Treatise, secs. 87, 88, 110, pp. 163, 177.

4. Perry Miller, *The New England Mind: The Seventeenth Century* (Cambridge, Mass., 1954), 467–471.

5. Locke, *Two Treatises*, Second Treatise, secs. 123–131, pp. 184ff.; Thomas Hobbes, *Leviathan or the Matter, Forme and Power of a Commonwealth*, ed. Michael Oakeshott (Oxford, 1957), 219ff.

6. Nathan Dane, *A General Abridgment and Digest of American Law* (Boston, 1824), VI, 711ff.; Hobbes, *Commonwealth*, 190.

7. On the English background, see Julius Goebel, Jr., *Felony and Misdemeanor a Study in the History of English Criminal Procedure* (New York, 1937), I, xxviii; W. S. Holdsworth, *History of English Law* (London [1909]), III, 331–335. On the early colonial situation, see the cases in Susie M. Ames, *County Court Records of Accomack-Northampton, Virginia* (Washington, 1954), 2; Elizabeth Merritt, ed., "Proceedings of the Provincial Court of Maryland 1670/1–1675," *Archives of Maryland*, LXV (1952), 32, 158; and Richard B. Morris, *Studies in the History of American Law with Special Reference to the Seventeenth and Eighteenth Centuries* (New York, 1930), 242ff.; Dane, *Abridgment of American Law*, VII, 128ff.; Haskins, *Law and Authority in Early Massachusetts*, 118.

8. See Dane, *Abridgment of American Law*, II, 481ff., VI, 622ff., VII, 212ff.

9. "A Coppie of the Liberties of the Massachusetts Collonie in New England," Massachusetts Historical Society, *Collections, Third Series* (Boston, 1843), VIII, 233; Dane, *Abridgment of American Law*, VI, 684ff.

10. See above, 46ff.

11. See Increase Mather, *A Brief History of the War with the Indians in New-England* (Boston, 1676); Miller, *New England Mind Seventeenth Century*, 481ff.; *Federalist Papers*, nos. 11, 12, ed. E. G. Bourne (New York, 1901), I, 74, 79; Walton H. Hamilton and Douglass Adair, *The Power to Govern* (New York [1937]), 70ff., 83, 99, 101ff.

12. John Cotton, "A Letter to Lord Say and Sele," Thomas Hutchinson, *History of the Colony and Province of Massachusetts Bay* (Boston, 1795), I, App. III; "Liberties of the Massachusetts Collonie," 232; Dane, *Abridgment of American Law*, VI, 664ff.

13. Mary N. Stannard, *Colonial Virginia Its People and Customs* (Philadelphia, 1917), 264ff.; Edmund S. Morgan, *The Puritan Family* (Boston, 1944), 78ff.; Emil Oberholzer Jr., *Delinquent Saints* (New York, 1956), 112ff.; Haskins, *Law and Authority in Early Massachusetts*, 61, 84, 89.

14. E. A. J. Johnson, *American Economic Thought in the Seventeenth Century* (London, 1932), 123ff.; Richard B. Morris, *Government and Labor in Early America* (New York, 1946); Dane, *Abridgment of American Law*, VI, 727ff., 744ff., VII, 33ff.

15. Noah Webster, *Collection of Essays and Fugitive Writings* (Boston, 1790), 36; Handlin, *Commonwealth*, 31, 53. For an example of the earlier clash of interests, see George L. Beer, *Origins of the British Colonial System* (New York, 1922), 156.

16. Handlin, *Commonwealth*, 67ff.; Louis Hartz, *Economic Policy and Democratic Thought* (Cambridge, Mass., 1948), 37ff., 82ff., 129ff.; Milton S. Heath, *Constructive Liberalism the Role of the State in Economic Development in Georgia to 1860* (Cambridge, Mass., 1954), 237ff., 254ff.

17. See the petition from Oyster Bay, August 23, 1673, in O'Callaghan and Fernow, *Documents Relative to the Colonial History of the State of New York*, II, 581ff.

18. Anson Phelps Stokes, *Church and State in the United States* (New York, 1950), I, 194ff., 339ff.; below, n. 23.

19. Handlin, *Commonwealth*, 113ff., 173ff.

20. Bray Hammond, *Banks and Politics in America* (Princeton, 1957), 369ff.; Joseph Dorfman, *The Economic Mind in American Civilization* (New York, 1946–49), II, 601ff.; Harry E. Miller, *Banking Theories in the United States before 1860* (Cambridge, Mass., 1927), 171ff.

21. Francis Bowen, *Principles of Political Economy Applied to the Condition, the Resources and the Institutions of the American People* (Boston, 1856), 22ff., 73ff.; Dorfman, *Economic Mind*, II, 512ff., 566ff., III, 370ff.

22. John S. Mill, *On Liberty and Considerations on Representative Government*, ed. R. B. McCallum (Oxford, 1946), 8, 10ff., 125, 138; also Samuel W. McCall, *The Liberty of Citizenship* (New Haven, 1915), 6, 27; UNESCO, *Freedom and Culture* (London [1951]), 11.

23. Stokes, *Church and State*, I, 518ff., 575ff., II, 5ff., III, 143ff.

24. See Herbert Spencer, *Principles of Sociology* (New York, 1891), I, 486ff., 536, 552ff.; McCall, *Liberty of Citizenship*, 32ff., 51ff., 54ff.; Richard Hofstadter, *Social Darwinism in American Thought* (Boston [1955]), 31ff.; Joseph Dorfman, "The Principles of Freedom and Government Intervention in American Economic Expansion," *Journal of Economic History*, XIX (1959), 570ff.

25. William Graham Sumner, *What Social Classes Owe to Each Other* (New York, 1883), 112ff. See also above, p. 63; Clyde E. Jacobs, *Law Writers and the Courts* (Berkeley, 1954), 27ff., 64ff., 128ff.; Benjamin R. Twiss, *Lawyers and the Constitution* (Princeton [1942]), 110ff., 174ff.; E. Burke Inlow, *The Patent Grant* (Baltimore, 1950); [Fritz Machlup], "An Economic Review of the Patent System," 85 Congress, Senate Judiciary Committee, Study of the Subcommittee on Patents, Trademarks, and Copyrights (Washington, 1958), No. 15; George E. Folk, *Patents and Industrial Progress* (New York, 1942), 15ff.; Harold G. Fox, *Monopolies and Patents* (Toronto, 1947); William B. Bennett, *The American Patent System* (Baton Rouge, 1943); John R. Dos Passos, *The Inter-State Commerce Act* (New York, 1887), 58ff., 69ff.; I. L. Sharfman, *The Interstate Commerce Commission* (New York, 1931–37), I, 19ff., IV, 170ff.

26. Handlin, *Commonwealth*, 26ff.; Ralph W. Emerson, "New England Reformers," *Works* (Boston [1903]), 256ff.; Stow Persons, *American Minds* (New York, [1958]), 153ff.

27. The most forceful statement of this position is in Henry D. Lloyd, *Wealth Against Commonwealth* (New York, 1894). See also the perceptive comments of Louis Hartz, *The Liberal Tradition in America* (New York [1955]), 232.

28. See David M. Schneider, *History of Public Welfare in New York State* (Chicago [1938]), 233ff.; Sophonisba P. Breckenridge, *Illinois Poor Law and Its Administration* (Chicago [1939]), 18ff.; Albert Deutsch, *The Mentally Ill in America* (New York, 1949), 132ff.

29. See, for example, the discussion of legislation on manners, Mill, *On Liberty*, 86ff.

30. See Mill, *On Liberty*, 95ff.; Lawrence A. Cremin, ed., *The Republic and the School. Horace Mann on the Education of Men* (New York [1957]).

31. George Rosen, *A History of Public Health* (New York, 1958), 240ff.; John B. Blake, *Public Health in the Town of Boston 1630–1822* (Cambridge, Mass., 1959), 167ff.; John A. Krout, *The Origins of Prohibition* (New York, 1925), 262ff.; Herbert Asbury, *Sucker's Progress. An Informal History of Gambling* (New York, 1938), 95ff.

32. UNESCO, *Freedom and Culture*, 7, 8.

33. Charles Nordhoff, *Communistic Societies of the United States* (New York, 1875); Arthur E. Bestor, Jr., *Backwoods Utopias* (Philadelphia, 1950), 38ff.; Donald D. Egbert and Stow Persons, *Socialism and American Life* (Princeton, 1952), I, 153ff.

34. Richard T. Ely, *Recent American Socialism* (Baltimore, 1885), 46ff.; Arthur E. Morgan, *Edward Bellamy* (New York, 1944), 223ff., 245ff.; Ira Kipnis, *The American Socialist Movement* (New York, 1952), 335ff.; Howard H. Quint, *The Forging of American Socialism* (Columbia, 1953), 319ff.; David A. Shannon, *The Socialist Party of*

America (New York, 1955), 76ff.; Dorfman, *Economic Mind,* III, 42ff., 149ff.; Egbert and Persons, *Socialism and American Life,* I, 267ff.; Richard Hofstadter, *Age of Reform* (New York, 1955), 225ff.; Arthur Mann, *Yankee Reformers in the Urban Age* (Cambridge, Mass., 1954).

35. Shannon, *Socialistic Party,* 150ff.; Egbert and Persons, *Socialism and American Life,* I, 308ff.; Association of Railway Executives, *Verdict of Public Opinion* (New York [1919]); Walker D. Hines, *War History of American Railroads* (New Haven, 1928), 230–237.

36. The desire for new revenue was a minor factor in the enactment of the income tax. See Edwin R. A. Seligman, *Essays in Taxation* (New York, 1895), 64ff., 311–314, 371–373; Edwin R. A. Seligman, *The Shifting and Incidence of Taxation* (New York, 1899), 307ff.; Charles A. Barker, *Henry George* (New York, 1955), 508ff.; also John Stuart Mill, *Principles of Political Economy,* ed. J. L. Laughlin (New York, 1887), 538ff., 555ff.

37. Lester F. Ward, *Psychic Factors of Civilization* (Boston, 1897), 96ff., 281ff., 313ff., 323; Herbert D. Croly, *Promise of American Life* (New York, 1912), 207ff.; John Dewey, *Reconstruction in Philosophy* (New York, 1920), 187ff.; Samuel Chugerman, *Lester F. Ward* (Durham, 1939), 319ff.; George R. Geiger, *John Dewey in Perspective* (New York, 1958), 163ff.; Persons, *American Minds,* 435ff.

38. Charles R. Van Hise, *The Conservation of Natural Resources in the United States* (New York, 1911), 370, 377. See also Rudolph J. Vecoli, "Sterilization: A Progressive Measure?" *Wisconsin Magazine of History,* XLIII (1960), 190ff.

39. *Theodore Roosevelt's Confession of Faith before the Progressive National Convention, August 6, 1912;* Croly, *Promise of American Life,* 172ff.; Brooks Adams, *The Theory of Social Revolutions* (New York, 1913), 47; George W. Perkins, "Business Man's View of the Progressive Movement," *Review of Reviews,* XLV (1912), 425ff.; Amos Pinchot, *History of the Progressive Party* (New York, 1958), 164ff., 248.; Eric F. Goldman, *Rendezvous with Destiny* (New York, 1952), 188ff.

40. Bernard M. Baruch, *American Industry in the War,* ed. R. H. Hippelheuser (New York, 1941), 15ff.; R. B. Kester, "War Industries Board," *American Political Science Review,* XXXIV (1940), 655ff.

41. A. A. Berle, Jr., *New Directions in the New World* (New York, 1940), 66ff., 96ff.; John M. Blum, *From the Morgenthau Diaries* (Boston, 1959), 229ff., 297ff., 345ff.; C. Herman Pritchett, *The Tennessee Valley Authority* (Chapel Hill, 1943), 116ff.; Hartz, *Liberal Tradition,* 270.

42. John R. Craf, *Survey of the American Economy, 1940–1946* (New York, 1947), 29ff.; David Novik, et al., *Wartime Production Controls* (New York, 1949), 35ff., 76ff.; John K. Galbraith, *American Capitalism* (Boston, 1956), 135ff.:; Stephen K. Bailey, *Congress Makes a Law* (New York [1950]), 228; Eugene V. Rostow, *Planning for*

Freedom: The Public Law of American Capitalism (New Haven, 1959), 66ff.; Oscar Gass, "Liberal Capitalism and Socialism," *Commentary*, XXX (1960), 49ff.

43. Frank H. Knight, *Freedom and Reform* (New York [1947]), 202, 339ff. For hostile views of these developments see Jules Abels, *Welfare State* (New York, [1951]); Sheldon Glueck, ed., *The Welfare State and the National Welfare* (Cambridge, Mass., 1952); for favorable views see Oscar R. Ewing, *The Nation's Health* (New York, 1948).

44. George Santayana, *Dominations and Powers* (New York, 1951), 58.

45. The absence of the feudal background is the theme of Hartz, *Liberal Tradition, passim.*

CHAPTER V. VOLUNTARY ASSOCIATIONS

1. Otto Gierke, *Political Theories of the Middle Ages*, trans. Frederic William Maitland (Boston [1958], 27, 94, 97, 98.

2. Henri Sée, *La France économique et sociale au XVIIIᵉ siècle* (Paris, 1933), 100ff.; George Unwin, *The Gilds and Companies of London* (2d ed., London [1925]), 155ff., 217ff.; George Unwin, *Industrial Organization in the Sixteenth and Seventeenth Centuries* (Oxford, 1904), 103ff.; Marcel Berthon, *Les Associations professionelles et ouvrières en Auvergne, au XVIIIᵉ siècle* (Clermont-Ferrand, 1935), 63, 71ff. For examples of the disabilities of religious practice outside the established church see Douglas Newton, *Catholic London* (London [1950]), 285.

3. Roger Williams, "The Bloody Tenent of Persecution" (S. L. Caldwell, ed.), Narragansett Club, *Publications*, III (1867), 73; Milton R. Konvitz, *Fundamental Liberties of a Free People* (Ithaca [1957]), 12ff., 19ff.

4. The classic statement is Alexis de Tocqueville, *L'Ancien régime et la révolution* (4th ed., Paris, 1860), 41ff., 69ff., 83ff., 107ff. See also Harold J. Laski, *Foundations of Sovereignty* (New Haven [1921]), 139ff., 171ff.; Harold J. Laski, *Authority in the Modern State* (New Haven, 1919), 321ff.; Joseph Drioux, *Étude économique et juridique sur les associations* (Paris, 1884), 269ff.; Berthon, *Les Associations en Auvergne*, 113, 114; Edmond Soreau, "La Loi Le Chapelier," *Annales historiques de la révolution française*, VIII (1931), 287ff.; Mathew H. Elbow, *French Corporative Theory, 1789–1948* (New York, 1953), 51–52; Ralph H. Bowen, *German Theories of the Corporative State* (New York [1947]), 24ff. Most treatments concentrate on territorial centralization but deal also, if incidentally, with the broader aspects. See, e.g., Hedwig Hintze, *Staatseinheit und Föderalismus im alten Frankreich* (Berlin, 1928), 41ff.; Otto Hintze, *Geist und Epochen der preussichen Geschichte* (Leipzig, 1943), 347ff., 434ff.

5. Joseph S. Davis, *Essays in the Earlier History of American Corporations* (Cambridge, Mass., 1917), I, 25ff., 75ff.

6. Davis, *Essays in History of Corporations*, I, 60.

7. James Bryce, *American Commonwealth* (New York, 1911), II, 763ff.

8. Thomas Jefferson, *Notes on the State of Virginia* (Philadelphia, 1801), 307ff.

9. Davis, *Essays in History of Corporations*, I, 96–103; George A. Billias, *The Massachusetts Land Bankers of 1740* (Orono, Maine, 1959), 32ff.

10. See, e.g., Richard Hofstadter and Walter P. Metzger, *The Development of Academic Freedom in the United States* (New York, 1955), 114ff., 187ff.

11. See, e.g., Thomas Paine, "Dissertations on Government, the Affairs of the Bank, and Paper-Money" (1786), *Works* (Philadelphia, 1797), I, 350.

12. Oscar and Mary F. Handlin, *Commonwealth* (New York, 1947), 113ff.

13. Handlin, *Commonwealth*, 233ff.; Oscar and Mary F. Handlin, "Origins of the American Business Corporation," Frederic C. Lane and Jelle C. Riemersma, eds., *Enterprise and Secular Change* (Homewood, Ill., 1953), 106ff.

14. Oscar Handlin, "Immigration in American Life — a Reappraisal," Henry S. Commager, ed., *Essays for Blegen* (Minneapolis, 1961); Oscar Handlin, "Historical Perspectives on the American Ethnic Group," *Daedalus*, II (1961), 220ff.

15. Handlin, *Commonwealth*, 144ff.; Charles Warren, *The Supreme Court in United States History* (rev. ed., Boston, 1937), I 474ff., II, 535ff., 562ff.; Edward S. Mason, *The Corporation in Modern Society* (Cambridge, Mass., 1959), 36ff.

16. See, e.g., Edwin E. Slosson, *The American Spirit in Education* (New Haven, 1921), 141ff., 168ff.; Elmer E. Brown, *The Making of Our Middle Schools* (New York, 1903), 279ff.; Lawrence A. Cremin, *The American Common School* (New York, 1951); Bernhard J. Stern, *Medical Services by Government* (New York, 1946), 18, 78ff.; James Rorty, *American Medicine Mobilizes* (New York [1939]), 74ff.; Harry H. Moore, *American Medicine and the People's Health* (New York, 1927), 23ff.; 36ff.

17. Bray Hammond, *Banks and Politics in America* (Princeton 1957), 326ff.; Handlin, *Commonwealth*, 173ff.; Louis Hartz, *Economic Policy and Democratic Thought* (Cambridge, Mass., 1948), 309ff.; Arthur M. Schlesinger, Jr., *Age of Jackson* (Boston, 1945), 115ff.

18. There is a careful analysis of the statistics in George Heberton Evans, Jr., *Business Incorporations in the United States 1800–1943* ([New York, 1948]).

19. For labor, see among the most important cases, Loewe *v.* Lawlor (1908), 208 U.S. 274; and Truax *v.* Corrigan (1921), 257 U.S. 312. See also Edward Berman, *Labor and the Sherman Act* (New York, 1930); F. J. Stimson, *Labor in Its Relations to Law* (New York, 1895), 78ff. For the business corporation see below note 20.

20. Among the works that supply material for a comparison see William Z. Ripley, ed., *Trusts, Pools and Corporations* (rev. ed., Boston, 1916); Eugene V. Rostow, *Planning for Freedom* (New Haven, 1959), 307ff.; Bishop C. Hunt, *The Development of the Business Corporation in England 1800–1867* (Cambridge, Mass., 1936); Karl Lehmann, *Recht der Aktiengesellschaften* (Berlin, 1898–1904); Rodolphe Rousseau, *Des sociétés commerciales françaises et étrangeres* (4th ed., Paris, 1912); Arthur K. Kuhn, *A Comparative Study of the Law of Corporations* (New York, 1912).

21. See, e.g., Roger M. Blough, *Free Man and the Corporation* (New York, 1959), 83ff.

22. See A. H. Hanson, ed., *Public Enterprise* (Brussels [1954]), 27–78; A. Z. Berman, *Municipal Enterprise* (Cape Town [1940]), 145ff.; Ruth G. Weintraub, *Government Corporations and State Law* (New York, 1939); Morton Keller, "The Judicial System and the Law of Life Insurance," *Business History,* Autumn, 1961; I. L. Sharfman, *The Interstate Commerce Commission* (New York, 1936); G. Lloyd Wilson, ed., "Ownership and Regulation of Public Utilities," *Annals,* CCI (1939); Ernest W. Williams, *The Regulation of Rail-Motor Competition* (New York, 1957); J. M. Bonham, *Industrial Liberty* (New York, 1888), 76–84.

23. See, e.g., John K. Galbraith, *The Affluent Society* (Boston, 1958), 251, 252, 309.

24. Foster Rhea Dulles, *The American Red Cross* (New York, [1950]); Clara Barton, *The Red Cross* (Washington [1898]), 36ff.

25. See Eckley B. Coxe, "Boards of Conciliation and Arbitration," Philadelphia Social Science Association, *Papers* (1871), 1ff.; Julius H. Cohen, *Law and Order in Industry* (New York, 1916), 32ff.; Julius H. Cohen, *Commercial Arbitration and the Law* (New York, 1918), 226ff.; Franklin D. Jones, *Trade Associations and the Law* (New York, 1922), 193ff.; also, above, 46. The implications of the role of government in compulsory arbitration procedures have never been adequately examined. Materials bearing on the problem may be found in Leonard W. Hatch, *Government Industrial Arbitration* ([Washington], 1905). See also Howard S. Kaltenborn, *Governmental Adjustment of Labor Disputes* (Chicago, 1943), 219ff.

26. William G. Sumner, *Folkways* (Boston, 1911), 177. See also Louis Hartz, *The Liberal Tradition in America* (New York [1955]), 11ff., 56ff.; John S. Mill, *On Liberty and Considerations on Representative Government,* ed. R. B. McCallum (Oxford, 1946), 4ff., 61ff.

27. See above, 118ff.

28. Jones, *Trade Associations and the Law*, 237ff.; Benjamin S. Kirsh, *Trade Associations the Legal Aspects* (New York, 1928); Benjamin S. Kirsh, *Trade Associations in Law and Business* (New York, 1938), 198ff.; Kenneth Sturges, *American Chambers of Commerce* (New York, 1915); Clarence E. Bonnett, *Employers' Associations in the United States* (New York, 1922); Benjamin A. Javits, *Business and the Public Interest* (New York, 1932), 52ff., 91ff.; Joseph C. Palamountain, Jr., *Politics of Distribution* (Cambridge, Mass., 1955), 31ff.

29. For partial listings, see Jay Judkins, *National Associations of the United States* (Washington, 1949), 561; *Encyclopedia of American Associations* (2d ed., Detroit, 1959), 198ff.

30. See Mason, *Corporation in Modern Society*, 40ff., 49ff.; Adolf A. Berle, Jr., *Power without Property* (New York, [1959]), 59ff.; [Community Chests and Councils, Inc.], *Yesterday and Today with Community Chests* (New York, 1937), 7ff.; F. Emerson Andrews, *Corporation Giving* (New York, 1952), 148ff.

31. The whole subject is obscure. Present evidence makes it difficult even to judge whether personality types change historically, and, if so, how, or whether the incidence of different types varies significantly from time to time. See David Riesman, *The Lonely Crowd* (New Haven, 1950); Erich Fromm, *Escape from Freedom* (New York [1941]); Clyde Kluckhohn, "Have There Been Discernible Shifts in American Values," Elting E. Morison, ed.,*The American Style* (New York [1958]), 145ff.

32. See William Kornhauser, *The Politics of Mass Society* (Glencoe, [1959]), 229ff.

33. Hammond, *Banks and Politics*, 740ff.; Lawrence A. Cremin, *The Transformation of the School: Progressivism in American Education* (New York, 1961), 127ff., 274ff.; Bonham, *Industrial Liberty*, 295.

34. There is suggestive material in Miles L. Colean, *American Housing* (New York, 1947); Martin Meyerson and Edward C. Banfield, *Politics Planning and the Public Interest* (Glencoe, 1955); Edward C. Banfield and Morton Grodzins, *Government and Housing in Metropolitan Areas* (New York, 1958).

35. See, e.g., Robert W. Fogel, *The Union Pacific Railroad* (Baltimore, 1960), 92ff.

36. Pierce Williams and Frederick E. Croxton, *Corporation Contributions to Organized Community Welfare Services* (New York, 1930), 94, 96; William F. Ogburn, *Recent Social Changes in the United States* (Chicago [1929]), 139ff.

37. See, e.g., "Report of Temporary Emergency Relief Administration," *New York State Legislative Document* (1932), no. 53, p. 17.

38. See, e.g., Carroll H. Woody, *Growth of the Federal Govern-*

ment 1915–1932 (New York, 1934), 403ff. 430ff.; Alfred de Grazia, ed., *Grass Roots Private Welfare* (New York, 1957), 281, 285; John Price Jones Corporation, *Philanthropy Today* (New York, 1949); Andrews, *Corporation Giving*, 173ff.; Richard Eells, *Corporation Giving in a Free Society* (New York [1956]); Adolf A. Berle, Jr., *The 20th Century Capitalist Revolution* (New York [1954]), 113.

39. Fredrika Bremer, *The Homes of the New World; Impressions of America* (New York, 1853), II, 152–154.

CHAPTER VI. RESTRICTIVE ASSOCIATION

1. See Arthur R. Burns, *The Decline of Competition* (New York, 1936), 462ff., 518ff.; Charles F. Roos, *NRA Economic Planning* (Bloomington, Ind., 1937), 36ff., 45ff., 563ff.; Leverett S. Lyon, et al., *The National Recovery Administration* (Washington, 1935), 83ff., 551ff.; also, above, 150ff.

2. Emil Oberholzer, Jr., *Delinquent Saints* (New York, 1956), 22ff., 200; Edmund S. Morgan, *The Puritan Dilemma: the Story of John Winthrop* (Boston [1958]), 150.

3. Ralph V. Harlow, *Samuel Adams* (New York, 1923), 8ff., 79ff.; H. B. Dawson, *Sons of Liberty in New York* (New York, 1859); Charles W. Ferguson, *Fifty Million Brothers* (New York [1937]), 20ff.; Henry Whittemore, *Free Masonry in North America* (New York, 1889); James D. Carter, *Masonry in Texas* (Waco, 1955), 21ff.

4. See, in general, Serge Hutin, *Histoire mondiale des sociétés secrètes* (Paris [1959]); Herbert Vivian, *Secret Societies* (London [1927]). *United Sons of Industry Illustrated* (Chicago, 1881) is a typical manual. See also Noel P. Gist, *Secret Societies* (Columbia, Mo., 1940), 80–155.

5. See, in general, Albert C. Stevens, *Cyclopaedia of Fraternities* (New York, 1899); Ferguson, *Fifty Million Brothers;* Arthur M. Schlesinger, "Biography of a Nation of Joiners," *American Historical Review*, L (1944), 1ff.

6. See Richard B. Morris, *Government and Labor in Early America* (New York, 1946), 136ff.; Adam Smith, *An Inquiry into the Nature and Causes of the Wealth of Nations* (3d ed. London, 1784), I, 183ff.; Allan Nevins, *A Study in Power John D. Rockefeller* (New York, 1953), I, 210, 266, 267; F. J. Stimson, *Handbook to the Labor Law* (New York, 1896), 185ff.; Charles O. Gregory, *Labor and the Law* (2d ed., New York [1958]), 13ff., 105ff., 200ff.

7. Ferguson, *Fifty Million Brothers*, 108ff.; Eugene P. Link, *Democratic Republican Societies* (New York, 1942), 115; *Remarks on the Majority and Minority Reports of the Select Committee on Secret Societies, of the House of Delegates of Maryland* (New York, 1856);

Oscar Handlin, *Boston's Immigrants* (Cambridge, Mass., 1959), 192ff.; W. Darrell Overdyke, *The Know-Nothing Party in the South* (Baton Rouge, 1950), 34ff.; Hutin, *Histoire mondiale*, 346ff; Stanley F. Horn, *Invisible Empire* (Boston, 1939), 42ff.; Oscar Handlin, *American People in the Twentieth Century* (Cambridge, Mass., 1954), 153ff.

8. James W. Bryan, *Development of the English Law of Conspiracy* (Baltimore, 1909), 55ff.; Percy H. Winfield, *History of Conspiracy and Abuse of Legal Procedure* (Cambridge, 1921), 29ff., 96ff., 115ff.; Frederic J. Stimson, "The Law of Combined Action," *American Law Review*, XLV (1911), 1ff.

9. Stimson, *Handbook*, 222ff.; Harry W. Laidler, *Boycotts and the Labor Struggle* (New York [1913]), 69ff., 134ff., 151ff., 170ff., 180ff., 200ff.; Morris, *Government and Labor*, 206ff.; Leonard W. Levy, *The Law of the Commonwealth and Chief Justice Shaw* (Cambridge, Mass., 1957); John R. Commons et al., *Documentary History of American Industrial Society* (Cleveland, 1910), III, IV.

10. Sidney T. Miller, "The Case of the Monopolies," *Michigan Law Review*, VI (1907), 1ff.

11. Milton R. Konvitz, *Fundamental Liberties of a Free People* (Ithaca [1957]), 336ff.; Eldridge F. Dowell, *History of Criminal Syndicalism Legislation* (Baltimore, 1939), 45ff.; Zechariah Chafee, Jr., *Free Speech in the United States* (Cambridge, Mass., 1941), 343ff.

12. See [Daniel Horsmanden], *A Journal of the Proceedings in the Detection of the Conspiracy Formed by Some White People, in Conjunction with Negro and Other Slaves, for Burning the City of New-York in America, and Murdering the Inhabitants* (New York, 1744); Kenneth Scott, "The Slave Insurrection in New York in 1712," *New-York Historical Society Quarterly*, XLV (1961), 43ff.; Kenneth W. Stampp, *The Peculiar Institution* (New York, 1956), 134ff.; Wallace E. Davies, *Patriotism on Parade* (Cambridge, Mass., 1955), 6ff.; Vernon Stauffer, *New England and the Bavarian Illuminati* (New York, 1918); Abraham Bishop, *Proofs of a Conspiracy, against Christianity, and the Government of the United States* (Hartford, 1802).

13. Frank L. McVey, "The Populist Movement," American Economic Association, *Economic Studies*, I (1896), 201–202; Oscar Handlin, *Adventure in Freedom* (New York, 1954), 184ff.; *Minutes of the National Christian Convention Opposed to Secret Societies* (Chicago, 1868); David B. Davis, "Some Themes of Counter-Subversion: An Analysis of Anti-Masonic, Anti-Catholic, and Anti-Mormon Literature," *Mississippi Valley Historical Review*, XLVII (September 1960), 205ff.

14. Norman Phillips, *The Tragedy of Apartheid* (New York, 1960), 135ff.; Albert Falcionelli, *Les Sociétés secrètes italiennes* (Paris, 1936), 184ff.; Enzo d'Alessandro, *Brigantaggio e Mafia in Sicilia* (Messina [1959]), 135ff.; Antonio Cutrera, *La Mafia e i Mafiosi* (Palermo, 1900).

15. *Address of the Antimasonic Republican Convention* (Worcester, 1832), 8ff. See also Samuel L. Knapp, *The Genius of Masonry, or a Defence of the Order* (Providence, 1828); Henry Brown, *A Narration of the Anti-Masonick Excitement* (Batavia, N.Y., 1829), 211ff.; Henry Dana Ward, *Free Masonry: Its Pretensions Exposed* (New York, 1828); John Quincy Adams, *Letters on the Masonic Institution* (Boston, 1847); J. Blanchard, *Secret Societies* (Galesburg, 1850); Josiah W. Leeds, *Secret Societies* (Philadelphia, 1888); Carry A. Nation, *The Use and Need of the Life of Carry A. Nation* (Topeka, 1908), 66, 356ff.; Ferguson, *Fifty Million Brothers*, 22ff.; Charles McCarthy, "The Anti-Masonic Party," American Historical Association, *Annual Report 1902* (Washington, 1903), I, 365ff.

16. Handlin, *American People*, 203.

17. Handlin, *Boston's Immigrants*, 203ff.; Oscar Handlin, *Race and Nationality in American Life* (Boston, 1957), 183ff.

18. Nation, *Life*, 379.

19. Burns, *Decline of Competition*, 44.

20. Shelley v. Kraemer (1948), 334 U.S. 1; Jack Greenberg, *Race Relations and American Law* (New York, 1959), 279ff.; Charles Abrams, *Forbidden Neighbors* (New York [1955]), 217ff. See also Roos, *NRA Economic Planning*, 9ff.

21. Terry v. Adams (1953), 345 U.S. 461; Greenberg, *Race Relations and Law*, 57.

22. Nixon v. Condon (1932), 286 U.S. 73; Walter Gellhorn, *American Rights: the Constitution in Action* (New York, 1960), 163ff.; Arthur E. Sutherland, "Private Government and Public Policy," *Yale Review*, XLI (1952), 407ff.

23. Dorsey v. Stuyvesant Town Corporation (1949), 229 N.Y. 512 and (1950), 339 U.S. 981; Gellhorn, *American Rights*, 183.

24. See Charles S. Rice and John B. Shenk, *Meet the Amish* (New Brunswick [1947]), 6, 7; Charles S. Rice and R. C. Steinmetz, *The Amish Year* (New Brunswick [1956]), 138, 139; Oscar Handlin, "Historical Perspectives on the American Ethnic Group," *Daedalus* VI (1961); Everett C. Hughes, *French Canada in Transition* (Chicago, 1943).

25. See, e.g., the problems of group libel, Zechariah Chafee, Jr., *Government and Mass Communications* (Chicago [1947]), 116ff.

26. Sidney E. Mead, "Rise of the Evangelical Conception of the Ministry," H. R. Niebuhr, and D. D. Williams, *The Ministry in Historical Perspective* (New York [1956]), 229, 230.

27. See Raymond Aron, "Totalitarianism and Freedom," *Confluence*, II (June 1953), 8–9.

28. Konvitz, *Fundamental Liberties*, 102ff.; Sydney V. James, "The Benevolence of American Friends" (Harvard University Dissertation, 1958).

29. Handlin, "Historical Perspectives," 226ff.; Handlin, *Adventure in Freedom*, 36ff., 157ff.
30. See Chapter VII.
31. See E. Franklin Frazier, *Negro in the United States* (rev. ed., New York [1957]), 674ff.

CHAPTER VII. POWER AND THE WEALTH OF MEN

1. James Morton Smith, ed., *Seventeenth-Century America* (Chapel Hill [1959]), 10ff.; Oscar Handlin, ed., *American Principles and Issues* (New York, 1961), vi ff., 31ff.
2. See, e.g., Francis Higginson, *New-England's Plantation* (London, 1630); Edward Johnson, *Wonder-Working Providence*, ed. J. F. Jameson (New York, 1910), 198ff.; Cotton Mather, *Pietas in Patriam, the Life of His Excellency Sir William Phips* (London, 1697), 28–30.
3. See Andrew Carnegie, *Triumphant Democracy* (New York, 1893), 139ff.; James Willard Hurst, *Law and the Conditions of Freedom* (Madison, 1956); David M. Potter, *People of Plenty* (Chicago [1954]).
4. E. A. J. Johnson, *American Economic Thought in the Seventeenth Century* (London, 1932), 98ff.; Bernard Bailyn, "The *Apologia* of Robert Keayne," *William and Mary Quarterly*, VII (1950), 568ff.
5. Richard McKeon, "The Development of the Concept of Property in Political Philosophy," *Ethics*, XLVIII (1937–38), 302ff., 344.
6. See above, 76; Francis Bowen, *Principles of Political Economy* (2d ed., Boston, 1859), 27.
7. See Henry C. Carey, *Principles of Political Economy* (Philadelphia, 1837–1840); Bowen, *Principles of Political Economy*, 127, 128, 545, 546; William G. Sumner, *What Social Classes Owe to Each Other* (New York, 1883), 112ff.; Joseph Dorfman, *Economic Mind in American Civilization* (New York, 1949), III, 258ff.
8. John Taylor, *Inquiry into the Principles and Policy of the Government of the United States* (Fredericksburg, 1814), 274, 275; McKeon, "Concept of Property," 360.
9. Daniel Webster, "First Settlement of New England," *Works* (4th ed., Boston, 1853), I, 34ff.; Edward Everett, *Address Delivered Before the Mercantile Library Association* (Boston, 1838), 13.
10. George Frederic Parsons, "The Labor Question," *Atlantic Monthly*, LVIII (1886), 98–99. See also above, p. 184, n. 13.
11. Russell H. Conwell, *Acres of Diamonds* (New York, 1915), 17ff.
12. Seymour M. Lipset and Reinhard Bendix, *Social Mobility and Industrial Society* (Berkeley, 1959), 28ff.; Kaare Svalastoga, *Prestige, Class and Mobility* (Copenhagen, 1959), 356ff.; Natalie Rogoff,

"Social Stratification in France and the United States," Reinhard Bendix and Seymour M. Lipset, *Class, Status and Power* (Glencoe [1953]), 577ff.; David V. Glass, *Social Mobility in Britain* (London [1954]).

13. Oscar and Mary F. Handlin, "Memorandum on the History of Social Mobility" (International Sociological Association, Subcommittee on Stratification Research, September 17, 1959).

14. The Center already has under way two extensive statistical studies: one of colonial New England college graduates, their parents and children; the other of the career lines of Americans high in achievement.

15. On these problems, see in general Pitirim Sorokin, *Social Mobility* (New York, 1927), 117ff., 141ff., 164ff., 414ff., 463ff. For community studies that bear upon the problem, see Lipset and Bendix, *Social Mobility*, 147ff.; W. Lloyd Warner and Paul S. Lunt, *Social Life of a Modern Community* (New Haven, 1941), I, II.

16. See above, 114. For material on licensing, see Henry L. Taylor, *Professional Education in the United States* (Albany, 1900), I, 216ff., 496ff., II, 813ff., 1002ff., 1237ff., 1284ff.; Oscar and Mary F. Handlin, *Commonwealth* (New York, 1947), 72ff., 223ff.

17. Oscar Handlin, *John Dewey's Challenge to Education* (New York [1959]), 37. On the general problem see Lipset and Bendix, *Social Mobility*, 91 ff., Sorokin, *Social Mobility*, 169ff., 187ff.; Svalastoga, *Prestige, Class and Mobility*, 399ff.

18. Robert F. Seybolt, *Apprenticeship and Apprenticeship Education in Colonial New England and New York* (New York, 1917).

19. Robert F. Seybolt, *The Evening School in Colonial America* (Urbana, 1925); Handlin, *John Dewey's Challenge*, 21ff.; Paul H. Douglas, *American Apprenticeship and Industrial Education* (New York, 1921); Perry W. Reeves, *Digest of Development of Industrial Education* (Washington [1932]); Frederick E. Bolton and John E. Corbally, *Educational Sociology* (New York [1941]), 412ff.; Charles A. Prosser and Charles R. Allen, *Vocational Education in a Democracy* (New York, 1925), 220ff.; Charles A. Bennett, *History of Manual and Industrial Education* (Peoria [1926–37]), I, 266ff., II.

20. Thomas Woody, *Educational Views of Benjamin Franklin* (New York, 1931), 115ff., 142ff., 151ff.; Bernard Bailyn, *Education in the Forming of American Society* (Chapel Hill [1960]), 33ff.

21. See Omar Pancoast, Jr., *Occupational Mobility* (New York, 1941), 124ff. Some of these problems are treated for the recent period by Byron S. Hollinshead, *Who Should Go to College* (New York, 1952), 28ff., 135ff.

22. See, e.g., Frederick Rudolph, *Mark Hopkins and the Log* (New Haven, 1956), 65ff.; Bolton and Corbally, *Educational Sociology*, 76ff., 85ff.

23. See, e.g., Carter Goodrich and Sol Davidson, "The Wage Earner

in the Westward Movement," *Political Science Quarterly*, L (1935), 161ff.; Joseph Schafer, "Safety Valve for Labor," *Mississippi Valley Historical Review*, XXIV (1937), 299ff.

24. See B. H. Hibbard, *History of Public Land Policies* (New York, 1924); Roy M. Robbins, *Our Landed Heritage* (Princeton [1942]); George Nadel, *Australia's Colonial Culture* (Melbourne [1957], 10ff.

25. See Merle Curti, *Making of an American Community* (Stanford, 1959), 57, 77ff., 141ff., 179ff.; Sorokin, *Social Mobility*, 43ff; Bowen, Political Economy, 493ff.

26. See Bowen, *Political Economy*, 104ff., 129ff.

27. See Lipset and Bendix, *Social Mobility*, 101ff., 114ff.

28. Curti, *Making of an American Community*, 222ff.; Lewis E. Atherton, *The Pioneer Merchant in Mid-America* (Columbia 1939); Lewis E. Atherton, *Southern Country Store* (Baton Rouge, 1949); Lewis E. Atherton, *Main Street on the Middle Border* (Bloomington, 1954). See also Svalastoga, *Prestige Class and Mobility*, 394ff.

29. See, e.g., Seymour M. Lipset, *The Political Man* (Garden City, 1960), 367ff.

30. Arthur W. Calhoun, *Social History of the American Family* (Cleveland, 1917), I, 37ff. See also Lipset and Bendix, *Social Mobility*, 250ff.

31. See, e.g., Catherine E. Reiser, *Pittsburgh's Commercial Development* (Harrisburg, 1951), 125ff.; Richard C. Wade, *The Urban Frontier* (Cambridge, Mass., 1959), 203ff.; Natalie Rogoff, *Recent Trends in Occupational Mobility* (Glencoe [1953]), 64ff., 75ff.; Lipset and Bendix, *Social Mobility*, 104ff.; Oscar and Mary F. Handlin, "Ethnic Factors in Social Mobility," *Explorations in Entrepreneurial History*, IX (1956), 1ff.

32. Mather, *Pietas in Patriam;* Benjamin Franklin, "The Way to Wealth," *Works*, ed. Jared Sparks (Boston, 1836), II, 87ff.; Lipset and Bendix, *Social Mobility*, 81ff.; Kenneth S. Lynn, *The Dream of Success* (Boston, 1955); R. R. Wohl, "The Rags to Riches Story," Bendix and Lipset, *Class, Status and Power*, 388ff.

33. See Richard D. Birdsall, *Berkshire County* (New Haven, 1959), 25ff.; Dixon R. Fox, *Decline of Aristocracy in the Politics of New York* (New York, 1919); David M. Ellis, *Landlords and Farmers in the Hudson-Mohawk Region* (Ithaca, 1946); Neil A. McNall, *Agricultural History of the Genesee Valley* (Philadelphia, 1952).

34. Earl of Bellomont to the Lords of Trade, May 13, 1699, E. B. O'Callaghan and Berthold Fernow, *Documents Relative to the Colonial History of the State of New York* (Albany, 1856–87), IV, 516. For the professions generally, see Taylor, *Professional Education;* A. M. Carr-Saunders and P. A. Wilson, *The Professions* (Oxford, 1933).

35. Handlin, *Commonwealth*, 104, 138–139, 223–224; Handlin, *John Dewey's Challenge*, 35; Carr-Saunders and Wilson, *Professions*,

65ff.; Lawrence Bloomgarden, "Who Shall Be Our Doctors?" *Commentary*, XXIII (1957), 506ff.; Lawrence Bloomgarden, "Our Changing Elite Colleges," *ibid.*, XXIX (1960), 150ff. See also, for England, Charles Newman, *Evolution of Medical Education in the Nineteenth Century* (London, 1957).

36. See George G. Mercer, *The American Scholar in Professional Life* (Philadelphia [1889]), 13ff.; Birdsall, *Berkshire County*, 214ff.; Carr-Saunders and Wilson, *Professions*, 55ff.

37. For expressions of the ideology see Henry Adams, *Degradation of the Democratic Dogma* (New York, 1919); Irving Babbitt, *Democracy and Leadership* (New York, 1925); Ralph A. Cram, *The Nemesis of Mediocrity* (Boston, 1917); Ralph A. Cram, *End of Democracy* (Boston, 1937); Paul Elmer More, *Aristocracy and Justice* (Boston, 1915). See also David Spitz, *Patterns of Anti-Democratic Thought* (New York, 1949). The first effort at analysis, E. D. Baltzell, *Philadelphia Gentleman* (Glencoe, 1958) suffers from the inclination to accept the self-evaluations of the group.

38. Oscar and Mary F. Handlin, "Cultural Aspects of Social Mobility" (International Sociological Association, Working Conference on Social Stratification, December, 1957); Curti, *Making of an American Community*, 440, 441.

39. See Lipset, *Political Man*, 48ff.; Thomas W. Shea, Jr., "Barriers to Economic Development in Traditional Societies," *Journal of Economic History*, XIX (1959), 504ff.; Herbert Kisch, "The Textile Industries in Silesia and the Rhineland," *ibid.*, XIX (1959), 541ff.; Sorokin, *Social Mobility*, 508ff.; A.N. Whitehead, *Adventures of Ideas* (New York, 1933), 353ff.; John S. Mill, *On Liberty*, ed. R. B. McCallum (Oxford, 1946), 50ff.; H. M. Kallen, ed., *Freedom in the Modern World* (New York, 1928), 25.

CHAPTER VIII. QUESTIONS OF CHRONOLOGY AND CAUSE

1. Frank H. Knight, *Freedom and Reform* (New York [1947]), 23; Denis W. Brogan, *The Crisis of American Federalism* (Glascow, 1944), 42.

2. Alexis De Tocqueville, *Democracy in America*, ed. Phillips Bradley (New York, 1945), II, 318, 319.

3. See Aristotle, "Politica," *Basic Works*, ed. Richard McKeon (New York, 1941), 1221; Frederick J. Turner, "The Significance of the Frontier in American History," *Early Writings* (Madison, 1938), 219ff.; Walter P. Webb, *The Great Frontier* (Boston, 1952), 103ff.; Joseph A. Schumpeter, *Capitalism, Socialism, and Democracy* (New York, 1942).

4. See, e.g., Oscar S. Strauss, *Origin of the Republican Form of Government in the United States* (New York, 1885); William A. Orton, *The Liberal Tradition* (New Haven, 1945); Ralph B. Perry, *Puritanism and Democracy* (New York [1944]).

5. See, e.g., Samuel W. McCall, *The Liberty of Citizenship* (New Haven, 1915), 61ff.; Edward N. Saveth, *American Historians and European Immigration* (New York, 1948), 16ff.; Geoffrey Gorer, *American People* (New York [1948]); Max Lerner, *America as a Civilization* (New York, 1957), 355ff.

6. See Norman Buchanan and Howard S. Ellis, *Approaches to Economic Development* (New York, 1955), 405; Albert O. Hirschman, *The Strategy of Economic Development* (New Haven, 1958), 25.

7. See e.g., Walt W. Rostow, *Stages of Economic Growth* (Cambridge, 1960).

ACKNOWLEDGMENTS

Our earliest debt was due to the gentleman to whom this volume is dedicated. Arthur Wilson Page first conceived the idea of a sustained scholarly effort to describe the character of American free institutions; and he proved a devoted friend to the Center. We only regret that he did not live to see the appearance of the first fruits of a project close to his interests.

We have also become deeply obligated to those who shared the labor of planning and executing the work of the Center. Paul H. Buck aided us immensely with his wisdom and experience; and the members of the Administrative Committee, Crane Brinton, Paul A. Freund, Myron P. Gilmore, Carl Kaysen, V. O. Key, Jr., David Riesman, and George A. Smith, Jr., have been free with their time in discussing our problems and in reading our manuscripts.

We have also profited from the counsel of our colleagues Marshall Cohen, Donald H. Fleming, and Louis Hartz, who were good enough to discuss various problems with us. The members of the staff of the Center, in pursuing their own work, helpfully threw light on the general issues that concerned us. We wish particularly to recognize the assistance of Bernard Bailyn, Milton Berman, Daniel H. Calhoun, Norton H. Mezvinsky, Richard M. Brown, Clarence L. Ver Steeg, and Michael Harris. David V. Glass afforded us the opportunity to exchange views on some of these subjects with the members of the Committee on Social Stratification of the International Sociological Association of which he is chairman. We profited also from the helpful comments of Seymour M. Lipset and Willard Hurst. While this manuscript has thus had the aid of many scholars, we alone are responsible for the views expressed in it. Pauline Bender and Janice Shapiro efficiently prepared the manuscript for the press.

This volume and the Center's whole enterprise have depended upon the use of the unparalleled resources of the Harvard College Library and of its staff. We are particularly grateful for the patience of Douglas Bryant, Robert H. Haynes, and Thomas O'Connell, who have been untiring in their service to us.

The funds to support the work of the Center came from generous grants from the Carnegie Corporation of New York, the Eli Lilly Endowment, the United States Steel Foundation, the Kennecott Copper Corporation, the Sloan Foundation, and the Hudson Gas Corporation.

INDEX